thank, Steve

MY JOURNEY THROUGH MADNESS

by

Steven Wilson

the Peppertree Press
Sarasota, Florida

ISBN: 978-1-61493-474-5

Library of Congress Number: 2016917171

Printed November 2016

Contents

Preschool Years

Growing up, I was an unusual kid. My parents tried to mask the problem by saying, "Oh he's just a kid, he will grow out of it." I was always getting in trouble. Fights and being sent home to my grandparents was a daily ritual. Whatever my teachers wanted me to do, I would do the opposite. One of the memories I have is kicking dirt into the faces of some girls that were taunting me, mocking me for not hitting the piñata right.

I was first diagnosed with Sensory Integration, so anyone who touched me or even looked at me wrong was a recipe for disaster. Not fitting in was all right with me. I had such a vivid imagination that I could play by myself and not have a care in the world. The world was different to me—I thought that what I felt is how the world was supposed to work. Being diagnosed with three different illnesses was tough for me, because I didn't understand them completely.

Attention Deficit Disorder and Attention Deficit Hyperactivity-Disorder is what they said I had. Ritalin, Adderall, Daytrana, and Strattera became a habit every night or every day, and sometimes twice a day for some of the meds. I never thought in a million years that such an innocuous illness would turn into a nightmare. Preschool is kind of a blur for me, because I was so young, but the memories I have of it are quite vivid, even to this day. With my so-called Sensory Integration disease, I despised clothes, always running around naked, but luckily, that phase only lasted a couple years. I was so young, no one second-guessed what was wrong with me. They just thought, *Oh, this is natural*, but it wasn't.

One of my best memories was my dad giving me a Jurassic Park wristwatch for being on my best behavior and the smile they both gave me for the good work I had done. That was a great day—seeing my parents so proud of me for once—the first time I had a perfect record.

One of the teachers became so frustrated with me that she grabbed my wrist and squeezed with all her might. That didn't go well with my parents—they marched in and gave her a piece of their mind. My grandparents were never really upset with me, because I was so young, they just wrote it off as a normal-acting child.

I went to a Sarasota Memorial Daycare Center, because my mom was a registered nurse. My father was a lineman at Florida Power and Light and still is to this day. The reason they sent me to the center is because they thought going to my grandparents' house would put a lot of responsibility on them, plus, I wouldn't make any friends my age. I didn't care about friends at that time, because everything I did and liked, no one else did. The daycare wasn't all that bad, because if I got there early, the cook would always give me my favorite cookie—an animal cracker.

On the days I didn't go to the daycare, I would always watch, *The Price is Right*, with my grandma and is still one of my favorite shows. On the days my grandpa picked me up, my grandma would be right there asking about my day. When we got home, we would make tapioca pudding, which was one of my fondest memories as a child.

Grade School

In grade school, I wouldn't say I had *many* friends, but I had a few *close* friends. I would get caught up in my own little world and play by myself or find as much mischief as I could. I went through many girlfriends in that time period, but in the end, it was just grade school. I had many certificates on my grades and I excelled very well for the classes I was in. Typing was one of my favorites, because I got so good, I didn't have to look at the keys—this made my teacher very proud of me.

This is about the time I picked up my first book, *Stuart Little*. I fell in love with reading at that point and moved on to the *Goosebumps Series*. I still had my problem with being touched, so we went to my doctor and asked what we could do. I would take scalding hot showers and not burn me, but I would come out as red as a strawberry. She recommended a brush therapy, where I would have two hours of my day being brushed to calm my nerve endings or something like that.

Tabernacle Christian School, where I went for grade school, was a great school, but I was the problem child, always doing something the teachers despised. They had a disciplined setting called Tallies and four Tallies in a week was detention, which became a regular setting for me.

Third grade was the worse, because I thought the teacher was out to get me, which became to be one of my delusions. By fourth grade, I switched schools and went to Sarasota Lutheran

School, which was a good change for my parents and me.

I always knew I was different going through preschool and grade school, but I didn't even think about the sinister outcome that was coming my way. Anxiety, depression, and the feeling of melancholy was a daily routine, but I didn't know how to tell my parents without upsetting them. I had already been on all these uppers like Adderall and Ritalin, but it wasn't helping the underlying problem that I had.

My dad is a bodybuilder, the same as my mom, so I picked up working out. At first, I hated it, but soon grew to love it. Many days, I would cry about going into the gym, which we have in our back yard, and my paps would push me to work out saying, it'll help my problems, which it did, but that was only part of the cake mix.

We were starting to wonder if ADHD and ADD were even proper diagnoses. My medicine would hype me up and it would take a heavy dose of Benadryl to put me to sleep. It would not be until high school that I found out what I truly have, but we will get to that. I remember being very ill all the time from either taking my meds on an empty stomach or just feeling sick in general. My temper started to take a turn for the worse. Each day I felt annoyed and irritated and it kept getting more serious. My doctor at the time was a great doctor, but he just didn't have a proper diagnosis for me. My best recollection of my disease didn't start until high school, so I will skip middle school and go to high school.

Mania

WHEN I FIRST ENTERED HIGH SCHOOL, I WAS GOING TO a school called "Brickhouse Academy." It was a great school and my ninth grade year was amazing, but my temper and my mood were increasingly hateful.

At this time, I didn't tell anyone I was having delusions or hallucinations—I kept it all to myself, which only made matters worse. At night, I would see shadow people and I would be so terrified that I couldn't fall back asleep. I was feeling suicidal and didn't know how to tell my family, until they witnessed something very sinister in my arsenal.

One night, I was called by a restricted number, which I brushed off, but they kept calling and being an idiot, I kept answering. I was throwing the F bomb, cursing as much as I could, and that's what brought me to the hospital for the first time in my life. I vaguely remember the whole situation, but I do remember being in the hospital bed with my parents right beside me saying, "It'll be okay, you're in a safe place."

But I was far from okay—I was terrified of this new setting, so finally the nurse came in and shot me up with Haldol and Ativan. The next thing I remember is being escorted to the back of a police car, dazed out of my mind, and wondering what the hell is this shit?

I woke up to an argument going on in the next room, a nurse and a patient. I freaked out, wondering if I was going to be in this place forever. I was in Bayside Memorial, but it was the best psych ward in the world compared to the next place I went to. At Bayside, they had great meals and an excellent staff—I got along with them just fine. The phones were always available except for group time, which I attended once a day. No one walked with tennis shoes, because they take the shoelaces out—you could try, but it was very uncomfortable. Your shorts couldn't have string in them and the showers had no showerhead—the mist just came out of the wall. The door on the bathroom had no lock, so if you were doing your business and someone walked in like your roommate, they would see the whole show. I was so out of it one day that I took a shower and forgot a towel. Instead of running out naked, which I probably would have done, I just used all the paper towels and dried off after about a half hour. I would spend hours in a catatonic state in my bed, waiting for the psychiatrist to come, so I could get the hell out of there.

Finally, after I had been doing all the research I could about my illness and ran across Manic-Depressive Disorder, I met my first doctor. When I brought it up to her, she said we don't call it that anymore. We call it bipolar. By this time, my hallucinations were absolutely horrible. I would see shadow people, hear non-existent things, and even smell things that weren't there. I was diagnosed bipolar psychosis, because they thought my mania was the cause of all the hallucinations.

I was also deeply depressed and anxious, so I was put on Xanax and Zoloft. That didn't go too well. Then finally, I met a new doctor through a friend, who turned out to be my doctor for almost as long as I have been sick. Scott was my therapist ever since I was fifteen. He gave me a lot of helpful tips that I still use to this day. I was suicidal and didn't want to live anymore. I needed a helping hand and he was there for me the whole journey.

When we finally realized I was bipolar, I was put on Depakote, which helped, but I was gaining weight and died off soon after, so we stopped that and tried a new drug. I had a meltdown one day, so I went back to Bayside. Then they realized that they couldn't help me reach my full potential.

I was transported from the hospital to a place in Orlando called La Amistad. When we arrived, I got out and walked into the main front office about three miles from the facility. They asked their questions like, "Are you homicidal or suicidal?" Then about six hours later, I was being transported to the living facility.

I had already made a fast friend from the bus ride there to this non-familiar place. I was exhausted by the time I arrived, so I went straight to my bed and slept. I was upset not to have my friend as a roommate, but he was just across the hall. The next morning, I woke up to one of the counselors yelling in our room saying, "Morning exercise—time to get up!"

It was six damn thirty in the morning and I was not used to that. After group, we had breakfast and then straight back to groups until 4 o'clock in the afternoon. Then we had free time, which almost everyone (if not everyone) smoked cigarettes—I just had to be strong and keep away. I would spend my time reading novels and memoirs, like Kay Redfield Jameson and Stephen King.

It was always a good idea to be friends with the cook, because you could get extra, and he was a damn good cook. Every time there was a Narcotics Anonymous (NA) or Alcoholic Anonymous (AA) meeting, I would attend, so I could go on an outing, which was either to get cigarettes, coffee, or books and that was it.

You had to go around the room in the mornings before group and tell how you were feeling and pick a word for the day. I made the mistake of making Xanax my word of the day—that didn't go well, because a lot of people there were recovering addicts. So I had to go through the whole bit of apologizing and saying it'll never happen again.

It was nice to sit back and relax and listen to other people's stories on how they got there or what they have—everyone was very open there. I missed home so much and wanted nothing more, but to be back with my family.

I waited for about a week before the doctor arrived and called me into his office to decide my fate. What he said is what my mom had dreaded for a long time after she heard it—he wanted to start me on Lithium. My mom knew the risks and that's why she was so upset at first, but it was soon to become one of my charms. We started on a low dose and I was sent home. That was the happiest I had ever been in my life, freedom from these groups!

When I first got home, all was well. I wasn't sick for a while, but I was still having hallucinations. I thought that this was odd, because I wasn't manic, so why the hell was I still having these?

A few months afterwards—maybe a year or so—I was complaining about suicide, so my doctor sent me back to Bayside, where I stayed for a week to get some medicine changes. While I was in there, I read and watched some television, but mainly stayed in my room.

When the doctor came for my discharge, I knew I would be home once again, so this time I kept my illness to myself. That worked for a couple months, but then I hit a real low point. When I was taking Xanax—I wouldn't say I was abusing them— I built up a tolerance to them to where the more I took, the less it worked. We had a scare with that when I took way too much. It wasn't anyone's fault—I just didn't think they were working well. After all this happened, I had a suicide attempt—I won't say how, but I was low and called the suicide hotline afterwards. I don't know why, but it probably saved my life.

From there, I went to Bayside Hospital with a watcher to make sure I didn't attempt that again and was there for three days. I thought it was going to be a breeze, because of all the times I had been there, but then I heard those dreadful words, "You're going back to La Amistad." My heart sank, because I knew I would be there for a while this time. So I returned and went through the whole process again—six hours of paperwork and I was back as a resident.

Phone privileges were given around six thirty and with as many people as were there, you better damn well hope you get to the phone first, because many of those people don't share well, especially if they're talking to their family. If someone had money every now and then, we would order pizza and Chinese. You had to pay for it with your own money though, which a lot of people didn't have. I usually spent my time reading or with my new friend playing basketball or ping-pong. I missed my family—it had been two weeks, but I still have another three to go.

We were given chores to do around the facility, like mop, sweep, clean the ashtrays, wipe off the dining room tables, and more. The NA and AA groups were fun, because I got to listen to a lot of people's stories, even though I didn't share, because I have never been through that, but it gave me a lot of insight. The residents were a charm to be around, even though most were recovering addicts with a mental disorder. I was probably the only one there with no history of substance abuse.

The morning word was always the hardest part, because I didn't know what to say or do, so I would pick a random word that would suffice. I'm amazed that none of the residents had Chronic Obstructive Pulmonary Disease with how much they smoked—like a pack or two a day. One day, a new kid came and was playing basketball by himself, so I thought that I would go over and introduce myself. By the time I reached him, he started to hit some imaginary force, dropped down, and had a Grand Mal Seizure right in front of me. I didn't know what to do at first, but sit there and gasp, but I was able to reach the nurse and an ambulance got there in time. He was there the next day to play ball with. The day after that, I was sitting in group falling asleep—not because I was bored, but because I had so many drugs under my belt.

I couldn't stand it. Before I went to La Amistad, we had adopted a new dog only a few weeks old. I was one hundred percent positive she wouldn't recognize me, but that was the least of my worries. My main concern was getting the hell out of there.

My parents would come and visit me on the weekends—the only time they could, because I was in Orlando and they were in Sarasota. My cousin came to visit me, which was a nice surprise and I got to see his wife, too. They're a great couple, so I was especially pleased that he took time out of his day to see me.

Even though my hallucinations were still pretty bad, I wanted to leave this hellhole, but I knew it would not be wise. If and when I made it to the phone on time, I would always love to talk to my parents and my best friend—well, two best friends, a guy could ever ask for.

One of my delusions before I was diagnosed is that I thought I was in the Ultimate Fighting Championship (UFC). I would picture crowds around me, cheering my name, asking for autographs, and I bought some Mixed Martial Arts shorts, shirts, and a Warrior jacket with a UFC baseball cap. Crowds loved me—I was the new up-and-coming UFC fighter.

In 2012, the world was supposed to end, which sparked my other delusion. I would spend hours on the phone with the Help Hotline, asking them if they believed I was terrified and depressed—I just didn't want it to hurt one bit. Watching the movie *2012* and all these Mayan television shows didn't help, but I was frightened and intrigued all at the same time. No matter who and how they told me and explained that it was just a hoax, I still believed it and nothing could prove otherwise.

Before my illness, I had many girlfriends—they came and went and life moved on. I thought I was a ladies' man and in some cases, I was. After I became ill, all that went away. I had nobody to talk to or go out with, besides my parents, who are always there for me, and my two best friends. When I was put on Seroquel and Depakote, my weight skyrocketed to three hundred and thirty pounds. I was also on Lithium and Lamictal at the time, but those were debunked. Yes, they can cause weight gain, but nothing like the Depakote and Seroquel.

It was soon after that, I was prescribed antipsychotics. I believe that the first one I ever was on was Zyprexa, which helped for about two weeks or so, before I so-called "relapsed." Although Seroquel is an antipsychotic, I mainly used it for sleep.

My first ever full-blown manic episode I remember just like yesterday. I was addicted to coffee and I didn't want to let this high get away from me. I would have four or five cups in the morning and was set for the day. My workouts were intense and I thought I had been cured. I could do schoolwork with no problem and I felt smarter and more efficient in what I was doing—it was just incredible! It feels like meth mixed with cocaine or crack—not that I know what that feels like, but I'm sure it's pretty close, if not better.

That lasted for about two weeks, until I saw my doctor again. I was stoked, because I thought I was cured. I was still having hallucinations, but I thought, if I can feel this good, then I'm fine with that. I remember saying, "Doc, you got it—I'm cured!" But he knew right away what it was and somehow, I knew it was probably a bad thing, because what goes up must come down. Boy, I tell you I went down in the shitter fast! It was just the worst depression, anxiety, and I was afraid it would never end. I was wishing I was out of my own pain, but I can't leave it behind me, because it's my own brain doing this to me. I can't imagine how bad it could have been, because at the time, I was on Cymbalta, which probably reduced the effects of my depression, but it was still a living hell that I wouldn't wish on my worst enemy.

I was always afraid to have friends when I got sick, because I was fearful of getting let down or back-stabbed, so I just sunk into my illness and basically made friends with my hallucinations. At least the voices or visuals in my head would never let me down and they are always there. So basically I made friends with my so-called "problems" on my good days before I found my "cocktail" of medicine. When I had no problems, I would wonder where they were.

I met a beautiful young girl at La Amistad—she was charismatic and charming. We hit it off right away and would sit next to each other and chitchat about the most random stuff. She would have me write her letters every night before I slept.

Her smell of perfect perfume attracted me to her, but she was the jealous type, which I should have known from the beginning after she lectured me for talking to another girl. I would shower every day as she would, too, trying to get that certain scent of attraction. We would spend as much time together as we could. I liked her a lot, but I let it get in the way of recovery. I was too worried about the next time I could talk to her so that I pushed aside everything I had learned.

My therapist there warned me about "Love in La Amistad" and said that it never works out. When the counselors caught on to us, they made a speech in front of the whole group saying they didn't want to see any attractions there.

At first, I was furious. I was saying, "What the hell is wrong with these assholes, trying to tell me what to do and that I can't have a so-called relationship in this hellhole?" We didn't even pay any attention to that—we just kept doing what we were doing and it made the days go by fast as hell. I would go to as many groups as I could, even though I hated them, just to get my credentials. I needed to be discharged, and it helped the day go by fast.

When I first went there, I would have bizarre dreams. I dreamt that I had a stack of prescription painkillers that the college campus police were trying to get from me. I woke up to my roommate saying I had said all that shit in my sleep. I hated sleeping there, because the rooms were always freezing to keep the germs out and I had no jacket—just a damn sheet to cover up with. The hallucinations would frighten me to the point where I was sleeping with one eye open, thinking someone was actually there.

One of my roommates had Post Traumatic Stress Disorder (PTSD) and would wake up screaming in the middle of the night, jarring both of us awake. He had been in a gang and saw horrible stuff that no one should ever see. I myself was seeing horrible stuff, so I might as well get this out—I was seeing mutilated bodies, people hanging from the ceiling, little goblin creatures, and all the most horrible stuff you could think of.

The only way to get discharged was to be stable, which I wasn't. They didn't know, but I was a hell of a lot more stable getting out than when I went in. I had to receive a therapist's approval, as well as a psychiatrist's approval. I got right on the phone with both and three days later, I was heading home— again, hopefully never to return, even though it was a great experience.

I was picked up in my dad's brand new Ford F-150 and enjoyed the whole ride home. It's amazing how fast time goes by when trying to get home after a month in a hospital setting.

Even though I wasn't stable yet, I knew I could use the tools I had acquired at La Amistad. They would draw your blood every Monday there to make sure your levels are stable and to make sure the lithium was at a safe level. My levels were always perfect, so I never had to worry about it and I'm on a high dose of lithium.

Going back to my therapist, Scott, who helped me when I was fifteen, he taught me ways to channel that frustration and rage to putting it for something good, like working out or finding activities that I was good at. I was determined to excel in everything I do to be at my full potential. He helped with high school, taught me how to deal with normal school stuff, such as testing and good school attendance, which I tried hard, but sometimes I had to skip on the days that weren't important. Some will say, "Well, all school is important," which is true, but who wants to be there when all they are going to do is play activities that I am not interested in. I would do as much as I could with him. I even helped him move a patient's belongings from her house to her new Assisted Living Facility. Most of her books were sent to Goodwill—she must have had over two-hundred books. He was one of my role models in life and still is to this day, even though he has passed away.

My childhood therapist, Ruth, also has a great deal of respect in my book. She was a short, but smart lady, lots of knowledge in her field of study. Every time, I would sit in the waiting room waiting for her to call my name. She had a marble game where you build your own pathway of where you want the marble to go. I loved that game so much that I wanted to bring it home. I was always too upset to leave that game, than have to talk for a half hour to an hour of details I would have rather kept locked away in my cranium.

I never shared this before, but I was even having some sort of hallucinations back in the day. I just didn't know how to tell people without them thinking I was insane—we are all a bit insane in my mind. When the cacophony in my head was too much to handle, sometimes I would just sit and read and let the words float around my head as if being projected through my eyes onto the flat canvas. When I would enter her office, she had a dollhouse with everything a real house had: toilet, bedroom, living room, game room, and a basement or cellar. I liked playing with those, because it kept my mind busy and off track of what I was thinking.

We would also always play board games, like Chutes and Ladders, Cherry Pickers, or Monopoly, which was an adult game, but I believe playing it raised my IQ.

Back then I was still diagnosed ADD, ADHD. We would talk about my medicine, which wasn't working, because that wasn't the underlying problem. Looking back on it now, I think that I was always bipolar—we just didn't catch it in time to be put on mood stabilizers, but I was probably too young for that anyway. I had the symptoms of several different diseases, OCD, ADD, ADHD, or Generalized Anxiety Disorder (GAD). I had so much chaos going on, I didn't know what to feel, how to feel it, or what to believe.

The pills would make me very ill and kept me home from school on many different occasions. Or I would be so hyped up, I couldn't sleep so, I would take sleep medicine, but that wasn't the way to live life as a young child. During kindergarten, whenever naptime came around, I would always be yelled at or talked to very sternly by the teacher, but it wasn't my fault that I was like that—it was the meds. I just could not sleep and that would always get me in trouble, because I was breaking school policy.

Since I was in a Christian school, I was expected to do everything right and do what the Bible says and all that religious talk. I remember in third grade, my friend and I were messing with this girl named Christina. We were calling her a double fart and I was already on thin ice for my record there. The final straw is when I called her a devil fart. That earned me a school suspension and I had to be picked up by my grandpa, but he wasn't the person I was worried about—it was my father.

The ride home from my grandparent's house was a quiet one with my dad, but as soon as we hit home, he threw my lunchbox against the wall putting a hole in the wall, which made him even more pissed. I ran to my room and shut and locked the door, knowing he was coming with the belt—I got four good swats. I was in pain, but also furious, but what could I do? He's my father and it's his way or the highway to hell.

Middle School

I KNOW I SAID I WOULD SKIP TO HIGH SCHOOL, BUT there are some certain points I was to get across in middle school when I attended Brookside Middle School, "home of the barracudas." This is when the bullying started—I could not get a break. I was, of course, one of the smallest kids there, so I was an easy target. Even though I had been working out and doing martial arts, I could never see myself pounding someone's face in or kicking them in the jewels.

But there I was also a problem child. I received an in-school suspension many times and many detentions. I would go to the nurse's office and use the oldest trick in the book, the stomach ache and headache trick—that worked many times. It was one of those schools where you could wear any clothes you like—the only problem was that in sixth grade, I had to tuck in my shirt, which drove me nuts—I didn't like the feel of it.

Sixth grade is when my grandma died and I remember that day like yesterday. I was in P.E. and my coach said my parents had come to pick me up. I had a sixth sense about it, so I rushed to my locker, put in the combination, and ran to the front office. When I got there, my dad was crying, which he never does. He said, "Grandma died." I fell to the floor, begging it not to be true. But it was true. It was a long and agonizing trip to my grandparents' house. Luckily, I didn't have to see her body, which my mom says is only a vessel, the spirit has already gone to heaven.

Toale Brothers took her right away as fast as they could, because no one likes to see a passed-away relative. My grandpa said the night before she passed that she was in a lot of pain, she couldn't get comfortable, and could hardly breathe. In a way, I'm glad she passed, because her pain was over with. We don't know if she died from one of the diseases she had, Alzheimer's and lung cancer.

We had a hospital bed sent to their house to make her more comfy and I would lay in bed with her cuddled up, just spending as much time as I could with her, because I knew she didn't have long. She also had cancer in her butt, for which she went to radiation and chemotherapy. My grandpa didn't like it, because he said they were treating the wrong part. Her hair was starting to fall out from the chemo and she was a very vain person, so she quit.

One memory I try to forget of her, which I can't get out of my head, is when I was sleeping in bed next to her and she went to the bathroom and was naked, covered in feces. I said, "Grandma, I have to get grandpa." She said, "No, don't get Dick." I didn't listen, I went and got my grandpa and said what had happened, so he went in there to clean her up as much as he could. That was before she had the hospital bed—she wasn't comfortable in her own bed at the time.

One thing that made her happy was watching the *Price is Right* and making tapioca pudding. I wasn't a good cook so it would take me several batches to make the perfect one. When watching *The Price is Right*, we would always have a competition to see who could get the closest bid. She knew most of it, because she was smart at pricing things. She passed away on April 26, 2006 and at that time Bob Barker was still the host of the show, before Drew Carrey took over. That show was on from 11 to 12 and I always dreaded 12 o'clock, because her soap operas came on at that time and I hated those shows. Her Favorite was *The Young and the Restless*.

My grandpa and I would always watch westerns, and at times, my grandma would watch, too—movies like *Hondo*, *The Cowboys*, *Jeremiah Johnson*, and *True Grit*. We must have watched those movies a thousand times. When we weren't watching westerns, we would watch *Pee-wee Herman*, *The Big Adventure*, *Big Top*, and *Pee-wee's Playhouse*.

Before my grandma got bad off, I would sleep in her room with her and always argue about putting the nightlight on, because I was seeing shadow people. If I had the light on, it would help, because I could realize it wasn't true.

She had a subscription to a magazine called *Home Cooking* that I would like to read. One of the main reasons I liked it was because they had a scavenger hunt. They hid a small toothpick in the magazine—I always used to love the hunt. Every one of her magazines were marked where I found the toothpick.

We would sometimes watch horror films, *Child's Play* (one, two, and three), which was the Chucky doll films. I would stay up late to watch the *SyFy* feature presentation horror flicks. Even though back then they scared the living hell out of me, I still couldn't look away from the screen. I would always feel safe, because I had my pillow—a blue pillow with a white pillowcase—I would love to suck my thumb and rub my pillow. I was very young at the time that I was watching these horror movies, which is why I had a safe pillow. I would carry that pillow everywhere, Publix, Wal-Mart, restaurants—everywhere. My mother made it for me, which made it even more special.

When I wasn't with my grandma watching TV, I would go into my grandpa's workshop. He would teach me how to solder and make things. To this day, those are some of my best memories. He also showed me how to sharpen knives, too.

Back then, when I was able to eat grapefruits, we would pick them fresh from the tree, carve them up, put sugar on them, and eat the delicious fruit. I can't eat them now, because of the lithium

My grandpa helped me come in second place in the science fair for creating a light bulb—a small one—using lemons and zinc and copper. I don't know how it works, but it did and won me a ribbon.

He would also sit down and show me maps and a globe. He taught me how to add and subtract and also how to multiply numbers, which brought me ahead in my class at school.

One of my best memories I have is when he would take me fishing. I would catch every single fish in the ocean. Even though we were on shore, I didn't care how small the fish was—it was always a thrill. He would bait my hook with squid tentacles and that was like a fish's best friend. I don't know why they liked it so much, but all I knew is it worked.

When my grandma was alive, my grandparents used to come to all my school settings, Grandparents Day and everything they were there. They would always pick me up from school, because my parents would work so late—my dad sometimes worked 3-11 and my mom until five.

My mom would always take me to school in the morning before she went to work. Sometimes before class, my mom would sit in with me and play finger football. I would make a triangle paper fake football, create a goal with my fingers, and try to flick it into the goal.

When my mom got off work, she picked me up from my grandparents' house. We would go home and she would sometimes play Mario Brothers with me.

By this time, I had met my best friend, Chris, and we would hang out every day in school and out, he would go with me to my grandparents and my house to play Brute Force, Mario, and watch *Power Rangers* and *Pee-wee*. He lived down the block from me, where we could walk to each other's houses. I would go to the pool with him and I remember going to the beach with him to run a mile. I was always astounded at how fast he could run a mile.

He went to Tabernacle with me—that's where I met him for the first time in my class—we hit it off right away. I had many friends, but he was always my best. We liked all the same things and had a lot in common. I would go with him to play tennis with his dad, who was an incredible tennis player and could have been in tournaments if he wanted.

When the fireman showed up to our school to do a demonstration, they set up a fake house fire, with smoke in the trailer they were using. We had to partner up to go through it, so Chris was my partner and we would always make the best time. When the school would have fire drills, we were always the first in line to get the hell out of that fake drill.

I used to play basketball when Chris came with me and I fell in love with it. I came up with the name of our team, "The Blue Tasmanian Devils." I was never really good at it, because I was so young, but I'm glad I didn't pick that as a sport for too long, because it died off as fast as it came. When I was friends with Chris, my backyard gym was just being built. We had some dumbbells, a barbell for bench press, and not much else, but we would later acquire more equipment for it.

Before our gym was built, my dad and I would go to a gym on 12th Street to work out. I couldn't work out, because I was way too young, but I always found it fascinating to watch everyone lift weights. When the gym came under new management with a new owner, children were no longer allowed to go into the gym. At the time, I was quite upset knowing I couldn't watch my dad work out, but later I understood that no kids were allowed, because it was too big of a liability.

Usually when my dad went to the gym, my mom was still working, so I would once again go to my grandparents' house, where my grandma would make amazing pies—she was a kitchen genius. My grandma didn't know how to drive, so Grandpa was our chauffeur. We would go to Publix and Grandma would always get me blue cake icing to eat straight from the bottle.

We would eat over at my grandparents every now and then. Mom and Grandma would make the best food, which my mom still does, but my grandma was in charge of desert—strawberry-rhubarb pie was her best.

Grandma used to read me a book called *Little Critter* by Mercer Mayer. I also had a math tutor, who would come over to their house. We would always make jokes about her car. It was so loud and when it parked, there was a huge backfire. I felt bad for the tutor, because she was constantly trying to get me on track, but I was so hyper and unfocused, it didn't last long.

Grandma's wish was to be cremated, so we did and her urn still sits on Grandpa's table shelf with a picture of her and I together, right next to it. My grandparents' wish is to be cremated together and buried next to each other, but we might keep both in our house on a special table.

I had a nanny named Ms. Mona that I would see anytime I wanted, if I wasn't at my grandparents' house. Either I would go to her house or she would come to mine. We got along so well and she had a husband named Bob, who was always sleeping. We pretty much had the whole house to ourselves. She had many cats, which I loved, because they were so friendly. She was very nice to be able to keep up with my hyper self.

She brought me to a couple places where she was babysitting, but I didn't care, because I just loved her company. I remember going to this one house where she was babysitting, and this younger kid and I would just cause a ruckus and get on her nerves. Many times, we got a ping-pong paddle to the butt. On the days Mona had to leave the house for a bit, her older daughter Trisha would take care of me, but that was rare. She had an old station wagon, which was like a tank that I loved to ride in, because it felt so safe. But like in preschool and kindergarten, when she tried to get me to take a nap, I would always get right back up and go see her. She never got mad—I'm sure a little frustrated—but never mad.

I was never allowed to watch horror movies or movies with a lot of cursing, but my favorite G-rated movie was called, *Gold Diggers of Bear Mountain*. I was used to action-packed or horror movies and my favorite hero of action-packed was Arnold Schwarzenegger. I watched *Jaws* about a dozen times and hated the water so much, I would cry not to go in—at the beach that is—I was fine with swimming pools, but I always had the thought of a shark being in the pool. I was afraid of the drain at the bottom of the pool for some reason—I always thought a blob of matter would come and get me, but with Mona, I always knew I was safe.

She would take me to this girl's house who was a diabetic and her parents had a lot of money. Mona and I would play putt putt golf at that house on the girl's own little range. Mona would take me to her church every once in a while where she ran a Sunday school. I had fun there, but they were just little kids. I was a kid at the time, too, but I found myself far more superior.

My hallucinations at the time were starting to develop rapidly—the shadow people seemed so real, I would even try talking to them. I couldn't tell if they were men or women. All I knew is that I was seeing things that weren't there. I never told my mother or father, because I was afraid of what they might do, which was to send me away for a while until things settled down. I didn't even tell Mona, so who could I tell that I was seeing things that weren't there?

The first hallucination I ever had is when I was sitting at a restaurant called Honeytree. We were sitting down eating our meals and a flock of birds flew by. I told Mom that time, because she thought it was from the medicine I was on, Lexapro. After that, all visual and auditory hallucinations I kept to myself.

One night I was sleeping in the guest bedroom and my mom was with me, because I hated the dark. When I woke up to her not being there, I was scared and what happened next was the worst—I saw Chucky, the doll, sitting next to me. I ran out and got my mother, who helped me the rest of the night.

Every time my poor mother got settled in her own room, I would wake up to her not being there. Then I would always yell from the other end of the house to wake her up and come back to bed. We had a double bed in the room at the time so she had her own bed in my room, too.

I always have to have someone with me. At the time when my mom wanted to sleep in her own bed, I would have my dog. If I was hallucinating and didn't wake up the dog, I knew it wasn't real.

Finally, after my hallucinations had settled, we went on a trip to Las Vegas. Mona was with us on these trips, so my parents could go out to the casino and play poker, black jack, and slots. We were staying at the Circus Circus, which was a beautiful hotel, and they had an indoor amusement park with a roller coaster, to which Mona took me many times. Mona must have been in her forties, but sadly looked a bit older than she was.

Back to my father, who is a tall 6'2" man, huge muscles, and a good personality, and who taught me everything about bodybuilding. Because he worked for FPL, I barely got to see him, because of his hours—he would sleep during the day and work at night. When I did see him, we had the best times. Finally, when he worked the 7-3 shift, by the time he got home, I was home from school, so we would work out like crazy.

He had a botched surgery when he was twenty-one, where the doctor (like an idiot) took out his cartilage, instead of addressing the source of the problem. The first twenty years he was pain free, but as he got older the shoulder, which was basically bone on bone, finally created a crater in his shoulder. He was in so much pain, he couldn't sleep at night. Even through all that pain, he still worked as hard as he could and then would still work out, ignoring the soreness and pain he was in.

When he had his second surgery and was home until he recovered, he would pick me up from school—I loved to see him.

He had scar tissue removed, thinking it would fix the problem, but it didn't. It helped for a couple of weeks, but then the pain came right back. All he could take was anti-inflammatory medicine, because his job didn't allow him to take painkillers. He worked on power lines, so he had to be extremely careful and pay full attention.

No matter how close I was to my dad, I still kept my problems to myself—I didn't know how to explain it to anyone. I was hearing a cacophony of voices, some of which were so sinister, I thought I was going to die. I didn't even tell my therapist, Ruth, at the time, but I still kept it to myself. She was a good therapist, but there was no connection between us. I liked the games we played, but that was about it.

My dad is the strongest person I've ever met—he was and still is my idol. I always wished I were as tough as he was, but he was hard to match. My mother was easier to open up to, because she is in the medical field. At that time, she was a registered nurse and worked in nephrology, cardiac, and intensive care. She was very smart like my dad and she would go to all my appointments for the psychiatrist. She is also the one who did brush therapy for me, for my sensory integration problem.

My dad always said he wished he would have been a cop, but I'm glad he didn't, because that is a very dangerous job, as was FPL, but he was used to that danger. My dad never went to college, but he studied for four years school to become a lineman. He first started as a meter reader and worked his way up to a lineman. When he brought his huge bucket truck home, he would always take me up in the air as far as it could go—at that time, I wasn't afraid of heights.

My hallucinations were pretty bad at the time and finally, when I told my mom I saw birds in the café, we went straight back to Doctor Ramony, but we finally were at an impasse, since he didn't know what else to do. None of my meds were working, because I was probably a bipolar-type schizoaffective at the time, but it was difficult to know when I was so young.

My mom grew up in Detroit, Michigan, and her mother and father (my grandparents on my mom's side of the family) were raging alcoholics. My grandma was the mean type and my grandpa was the sad one. I knew him pretty well, but my grandma I didn't know as much as I wish I had. My mother was abused by my grandma, but never by my grandpa. Mom said she was always having to go with her sister, my Aunt Teri, to pick them up at the bar—two young girls having to pick up their parents is something no one should ever have to go through. Especially considering how young they were, they would take screwdrivers with them as protection. My grandpa was a fireman and a very good one, even though he was an alcoholic. They were also heavy smokers—Mom always told me stories about when they had to clean the dishes, my grandparents would put their butts on the plates, so my mom and aunt would always have to clean that off, too.

My mom had to walk in the snow to school and to this day, she still couldn't imagine what she smelled like from all the cigarettes they smoked in the house. Pretty much every family member on my mom's side of the family was an alcoholic. My grandpa would go through a case of beer in less than a day, while my grandma was the liquor drinker and would abuse my mother by throwing things at her and stuff like that.

When Mom and my grandparents moved down to Venice, she attended Venice High School. Before that, when she was about fourteen, she worked at a restaurant called "Kiss 'N Cousins." When my mom was seventeen or eighteen, she went to get her Certified Nursing Assistant (CNA) license. She used to tell me stories about being in school to become a Licensed Practical Nurse (LPN)—Grandpa would always make her Spam sandwiches with a pickle. He was always there for my mom when she needed him—he just had a bad illness. When he got off work from the firehouse, he would go straight to the bar and then come home to my mother crying, because he was a sensitive drunk.

My Uncle Chester was an alcoholic and my Aunt Mary loved to drink, too, but she never had a problem with alcohol. My mom was a strong person for never getting caught up in alcohol. She and her roommate would always go to the bar to get something to eat and when her roommate drank, my mom was the driver, because she never drank.

The funny part is that she met my dad in a bar, O'Toole's, which was also a restaurant. She said she saw this big handsome man, so well-dressed and standing at the door. When she went to the bouncer and asked who he was, he said, "Oh, that's Steve— he works at Florida Power and Light. My mom was instantly attracted to this stranger. She went up to Dad, asked his name, and they hit it off. They exchanged numbers—at the time, only landlines were available, because cell phones weren't invented yet. My dad told her he would call her at seven, so she raced home, but a police officer pulled her over on the way. My mom said, "Just give me the ticket." The officer didn't argue, but wrote the ticket, just in time to get home, so she could answer Dad's call.

After they had moved in together, Dad bought her a new nightgown and asked her to check the pockets to make sure there was nothing in there. At first, she hesitated saying, "I'm sure there is nothing in the pockets, but my dad insisted. When she looked, she found a diamond ring and he asked her to marry him. Of course, she said yes.

When she was pregnant the first time, they were going to call the baby, Andrew, but he was a miscarriage. When they tried to have a baby again, I was born—8 pounds 4 ounces at 7:03 in the morning—three weeks early. At that time, my grandparents were still alive, so they would come over to watch me play and enjoyed every bit of it.

I was spoiled by my grandma and grandpa on my dad's side of the family. My grandma would never put me in my crib—she was always holding me, which is probably why I never wanted to be alone. If I wasn't with her, I would be on the couch with Gramps trying to take a nap, but he never could, of course.

Growing up, I loved to read—my favorite books were true crime books. I wanted to be an FBI profiler, big dream for such a little kid. I also had a journal, which I kept a log of each day, but since I was young, the words didn't match up to what I was doing. I had a favorite tree that I would climb to the very top to sit on a branch and write.

I liked to watch scary movies like *Jurassic Park* and *The Lost World*, but those movies terrified me—even in the daytime. I remember thinking there was a velociraptor under my bed, so I would lunge to the door when I had to go to the bathroom. I would turn on the room light, hurry to the bathroom, and run back. When I turned off the light, I would run back, so it couldn't get me. I would always be afraid of my room, because I would see stuff crawling on the walls when I would try to sleep. Even when I turned on the lights, they didn't go away—they just multiplied.

My mom's folks were John and Sharon, and my dad's were Dick and Dixie. Since she was an alcoholic, Grandma Sharon had dementia that would later kill her. Grandpa John was a very smart man and could put together five-thousand-piece jigsaw puzzles, but that's pretty much all he had to look forward to.

Before Grandpa John died, he didn't want me to see him, because he was in such bad shape. In a way, I was mad, but he saved me a lot of pain by me not seeing him on his deathbed. The night he died, my parents went to see him and I said I wanted to go, too, because he was going to die, but my parents paid no attention to that. A couple of hours later after they returned home, they got the horrible call saying he had passed away.

I got to see the good side of Grandma Sharon before she died. She was a nice lady in the end—luckily, she remembered my name and who I was. I always held a grudge against her for what she did to my mom, but I forgave her and so did my mom.

She wasn't a mean-spirited lady, she just had a bad disease and her drinking didn't help her mood. My mom to this day thought Grandma Sharon was bipolar. Since it skips a generation, that's probably where I got it from, but I know of no one in my family who was schizophrenic.

A memory I have that I still cherish to this day is when my parents bought me a go-cart. I would ride that thing all over my yard, kicking up dirt and creating dead spots in the grass. Dad would take me around the neighborhood—at full speed, it probably went 25 mph, but it felt like 50. My friends, Brad and Taylor, would take turns driving it until Brad crashed into the fence—that's when we decided that I should be the only driver from then on. When I would drive around my house, I would see people standing in the middle of my pathway. It scared me so much that I would park and run inside to the company of my parents.

At the time, I thought it was just a blip. Whenever my parents asked me what was wrong, I would tell them nothing, but they knew better. At the time, we thought it was my medicine, Adderall and Ritalin, that was making me hallucinate. Even though I saw people in my way when I would drive my go-cart around, it always soothed me knowing I could ride for hours.

I probably pissed my neighbors off, because it was loud and I would drive for long periods at a time, but I didn't care, because I loved it. It was yellow and black and had a roll cage, but it was impossible to tip over. I would cut sharp corners going full speed and it didn't even go on two wheels. I loved watching the dirt kick up as I spun around the corners. It was only a two-seater, so we would have to take turns, if Mom wanted to drive on the streets with me. I was too young at the time to drive on the road, but I didn't care—I loved the ride. It was so loud, because it had a gas engine, and it was good experience, because it helped me to learn how to drive without having to take the car out and risk getting Dad in trouble with the law. He would let me drive his truck around the yard and that gave me even more experience learning how to drive a big truck.

My nanny, Mona, would crank the go-cart up for me and would sometimes ride with me, even though she was probably scared as hell letting a young kid drive her around going full speed. When I wasn't on the cart, I would watch G-rated movies with her, but I wanted to watch *The Terminator* or *Child's Play* with Chucky.

I was still in Tabernacle at the time and my parents sometimes made me go to summer camp, which was fun. I would play air hockey and some video games, but mainly we went on outings to Sun-N-Fun to swim or play miniature golf. I never swam, because I hated chorine—it would always burn my eyes, plus, I didn't want to take my shirt off.

I was in the bathroom with one of my bullies at the time and he wouldn't let me through to get out. I called him an A-hole and got banned from doing any activities that day—what else could I do since he had me trapped? Like a fool, he ran right to the counselor and snitched on me. Another reason I never swam there is because I didn't feel safe. Even though Grandma Dixie had a chlorine pool, I felt safe there and always swam in their pool—I just didn't open my eyes underwater. I would always make sure Grandpa Dick was there to watch me swim, because I thought a shark was going to come through the drain and eat me. I had watched one too many *Jaws* movies, but I still felt safe.

Mona wouldn't even let me play 007 James Bond, because there was a lot of killing in that game, but as soon as she left, I'd sit right in front of my TV and play. When we went to Las Vegas, Mona took me to a place called Excalibur, which was a knight show and we had to eat chicken with our fingers instead of forks. When the knights came out, one was riding a unicorn and I was thinking that this couldn't be real. But to me, it *was* real and I couldn't shake it. Finally, unicorn disappeared and I was able to enjoy the show.

Next, I started seeing cockroaches all over the table and ground. I kept thinking, great, they're going to get into my food, so I closed my eyes and rubbed them a little bit, and when I opened them back up, things were normal again. I still didn't tell Mona because she wouldn't understand and so, she would tell my mom, which was a no go. I kept it all to myself, so I didn't have to go to a loony bin and away from my family.

My third grade teacher, Ms. Vanhorn, told my parents that when she would call to me on the playground, I didn't yell back. At the time, I was still having auditory hallucinations, which made it hard for me to hear her, because with all the kids yelling on the playground, I couldn't tell what was real from what was not. They took me to an ear specialist, who ran a series of tests and found out that, of course, I was not hard of hearing—I just had so many of my own voices mixed in with the voices coming from the playground.

My favorite visual back then was me swinging, when I saw across the field the Teenage Mutant Ninja Turtles running with automatic weapons and a T-rex at their side. I don't know why I saw it, but it made me laugh.

Tabernacle

I always liked Tabernacle—I thought it was a well-structured school, which is what I needed at the time. I liked the computer class and typing. We had typing games where you look at a screen, while sitting behind the wheel of a car, and you have to spell words as they appear on the screen. If you were too slow, the windshield would become covered with bugs and you lost. I was always good at that game, because I used to type on Grandma Dixie's old-style typewriter—I liked the sound it made as I typed. That was all we had basically, because computers were not that good back then.

We also learned how to write in cursive—not print—so I never knew and still don't know how to print, but cursive is better in my opinion. Grandpa Dick showed me how to add, subtract, multiply, and divide at a young age, so I was a little ahead of my class. We would have to learn Bible verses and recite them back to the teacher, which I liked, because I had a good memory. We would sit around in a circle and the teacher would read us Bible stories. My best friend, Timothy, and I would always cause trouble, like acting as if we had to blow our noses about a hundred times just to get up and get on her nerves.

Miss Merrill was my third grade teacher. I used to gel my hair, so she would tell me, "Now, I don't want you in the sand, so you don't get sand in your hair and make a mess." I would go straight to that sand pit and started doing flips in it, and my hair would become a mess, so she didn't know what to do with me. Once again, I was brought to the principal's office, where I received a detention and my most hated teacher goes, "Keep him off the playground for a week."

My voices were telling me to do all this stuff, but I was too young to resist the urge to try to fight back. By this time, I had started my martial arts class. The first time I went there, I fell in love—the structure and discipline there was the best and it got my anger out and used it in a good way besides fighting. It was called Hwa Rang Do. My instructor, Jessie, saw something inside of me and would keep me after class to show me the belt forms that would make it easier to excel to different belts. They would have sleepovers, where we would watch Kung Fu movies and order pizza and Coke or Pepsi. We would also go over our forms for different belts and I would learn a belt ahead, since Jessie would keep me after and show me. His daughter, Paige, was incredible at martial arts—probably because her dad was the instructor and would teach her day in day out. I had a crush on her at the time, but was a little intimidated by her. I mean, if I said one wrong word, I was a sitting target for her and her dad would have put me in my place.

When we entered the class, we would sit down and recite what was on the board, which was in Korean, but the words were all distorted and I couldn't read them, so I thought, oh no, it's still happening. I should have known that it would only get worse later on, but I just put on a good mask like nothing was wrong and went on living. I would turn off all emotions when I entered the dojo, because that was my sanctuary, so I tried to make the best of it. It's as if my reflection in the mirror wasn't me, but a stranger looking back at me and, of course, there were mirrors all around the dojo.

I started bodybuilding when I was around nine years old. That was the time I would cry about going there and at the time, I was starting to gain a lot of weight. I would play this computer game called RuneScape all day long. I was so worried about getting Rune Armor on my character that I just gave up with life. That was one of the reasons Dad wanted me to work out so bad— to lose the weight. When I first started, I couldn't even bench 45 pounds. I was a non-muscular kid and was very scrawny with a big belly and very out of proportion.

After my go-cart, we bought a white club car golf cart that wasn't as fast as the go-cart, but it sufficed, I would go with my parents around the neighborhood everywhere. We would go down this path where Booker Middle was and ride to Myrtle and Tuttle—we called it the snake path, even though we never saw a snake. Mona would drive me down there sometimes when she would babysit, but not much, because it probably scared her. Plus, the cart was so quiet because it was battery-operated that we could sneak into places undetected, like vacant homeless camps, until we finally got caught.

Nothing happened, except spotting a nice bum, but it still startled us. We would ride along busy roads on the sidewalk, but I was always paranoid we were going to get pulled over. For some reason, we never did, but we did know a police sergeant, Stan, a nice guy who would always bail us out of trouble.

It was about sixth grade when I started to get serious about my true crime books. I would write book reports about them and my teacher was a bit worried about me, to be honest, but I didn't care—I enjoyed it.

The day I got an in-school suspension in sixth grade, I remember bringing in the book, *Helter Skelter*, about Charles Manson and his followers. I read the whole book—it was either homework or a book, so I chose the book. I would play a movie in my head, which was always fun, because my hallucinations would take over at that point and create a perfect picture in my head.

This was my most hated year, because it was when Grandma Dixie passed away. I brought that up before, but I remember sitting in gym class ready to play dodge ball when I got the call.

Grandpa Dick told me a story about her driving once—they were on a non-busy road, thank god, but he said she went straight into the ditch and had to walk a couple miles to get a tractor to pull them out. He vowed never to let her get behind the wheel again, so he was her ride for as long as they were married. She also had no depth perception, so every time Grandpa Dick would pull out into traffic, even if no traffic was coming, I remember her yelling at him, which was pretty funny.

Their house had two bedrooms and two bathrooms. I would love sitting in the tub in the first bathroom, and although the other bathroom was in their room, I used it, too. Grandma Dixie slept in the main bedroom and Grandpa Dick would sleep in the guest, because he snored so damn loud, which he still does to this day. It's like a freight train passing by or being woke up by a loud gunshot.

Fifth grade is when I met my friend, James, who I still see occasionally, but not as much as then. We would always goof around in classes and get yelled at by the teacher.

I remember one day I went to the restroom and I looked in the mirror. I saw a sinister-looking woman, so I ran back to class without even using the restroom. I always had to make sure someone was in the restroom with me, even if I didn't know them. There were no urinals—just stalls—but if I knew they were there, I would feel comfortable.

We had an ex-cop as a coach for P.E. who I always liked. He was very strict, but I liked structure. My favorite game at that time was kickball, as I could wham that ball over the building we had in the playground. It was not too high of a building, but enough to make me feel proud of myself.

By this time, I wasn't on any medicine—just trying to get by each day. It was very tough, because not only was I hyper, which was probably mania at the time, I was also hallucinating. Like an idiot I kept it all to myself, even though the school therapist, Jen, tried to get in my head, but I never faltered.

Back in 4th grade when I was still at Tabernacle, every time I would go to chapel, which was a requirement for the school, I would see an angel descending from the ceiling and land on the stage. At first, I thought it was an act, but it wasn't.

P.E. at Tabernacle was always fun and we played kickball there, too. I remember in kindergarten, my girlfriend at the time (or my crush) and I were playing kickball and she kicked the ball so hard it whammed right into the coach's face and busted her lip open. I still remember how much blood Miss Beasly was spitting out.

She had a pet baby squirrel that she would bring in occasionally, but what I loved was seeing it run around from shoulder to shoulder. Every Friday, we had Show & Tell and I brought in my toy, a Screaming Stretcher, which they hated, because they said it sounded like it was in pain. Well, duh, that's the point!

Back to sixth grade, my favorite teachers were Timmons and Simoni. They were both marathon runners and in great shape. Timmons was the science teacher and Simoni was the history teacher. I also liked Dr. Lynch, the language arts teacher. We could bring in a book to read and recite the plot after we were done.

In Timmons class, we would mix different chemicals and try to get a reaction out of them. Luckily, we had a chemical shower and an eye-face wash, if anything were to happen. Nothing ever did, because she was such a good teacher.

In reading class at the time, my teacher, Lilly, had us read *The Tell-Tale Heart* by Edgar Allen Poe. I loved that story, because it reminded me of my hallucinations and I could actually fit into something. Obviously, I didn't kill anyone, but I could relate to the story showing where his paranoia came from and seeing that one eye that drove him mad. It also reminded me of my true crime books, because there was a lot of carnage in them.

I still turned out a good kid, even though some say kids shouldn't watch PG13 movies or R-rated movies—it will corrupt their minds and the same with books, but I was ahead of my class in reading. I was reading college level books.

I also like paranormal books like *American Haunting* and watching the movie *Blair Witch Project*. I also would be thrilled when school was over, because I could watch my favorite show, *A Haunting*. That was also probably why I got all those sinister visuals and auditory hallucinations, because if I would have never seen them, I would probably see the Teletubbies or Barney, but to be honest that would be worse in my head.

At Brookside, we also had teams, four classes in one team, and alternate between classes. It was probably about forty to fifty kids. It was nice though, because I was always around my friend, Tyler, at the time. He had Tourette Syndrome—he didn't yell curse words, but he had an annoying tick where he would jerk his neck. I didn't care though, because I knew I was messed up, too. I was an undiagnosed bipolar Schizoaffective at the time, but how were people to know, if I wasn't talking about it? Also, it's very rare to be diagnosed with that as a kid. If I would have been diagnosed at the time, I would have fit right into that category.

Lunchtime was always my favorite—Brookside had great food. My favorite was noodles and chicken with a roll. I would dip my roll into my mashed potatoes—it was the best. Plus, at lunch my friend, Ralph, would tell urban legion stories, which freaked me out, but intrigued me.

In science class, Timmons would always play Bill Nye, the Science Guy. It was hilarious and also educational. I always looked forward to that show. We also learned about global warming, for which they were strong advocates. I never believed it myself, but it was school and you don't get to pick.

If I were to choose, there would have been an uproar, because I would pick *Chucky* or *Jason Voorhees* or *Nightmare on Elm Street*. Then again, while I would sit in class, I would hallucinate even more. Bugs crawling on the wall, angelic figures, demons, and even Jesus Christ himself would appear. However, I tried to be as studious as possible with no one knowing what was going on.

The bathroom was always a scary situation, because we only had one for the whole team. When I would go to do my business, I would see weird markings on the wall, like words in Latin or something strange. I remember I was in the bathroom once and my voices were bad. They said, "You're not leaving us, you're in here forever with us, and with no one else." That frightened me, because I thought I was seriously locked in for good—it was such a relief to get out of there.

I had developed this illness called Trichotillomania. I would pluck my hair out and put it in my mouth out of habit and I would come home with no eyelashes and a bald spot on the top of my head.

After school, I was always excited to get home, because my friend, James from fifth grade, lived a block away from me. I would walk, ride my bike, or skate there (when skating was still popular). I couldn't even tell him I was hallucinating. He had enough trouble in his life, so I didn't want to add on to it.

He and his brother taught me how to play the guitar. I would spend hours playing, because I was hoping the busier I stayed, the less hallucinations I would have, but I was wrong. I would hear different music while I was trying to play and couldn't concentrate. I was pretty good at it, but I could only play the intros of songs—no solos or anything. My parents bought me an Ibanez guitar starter kit, but I had always wanted a Gibson SG. However, that was too much money and my parents knew the obsession would die down eventually.

Before that, I tried to pick up skateboarding. I bought a brand new board with blue grip tape—I loved that board so much. I saw my friend at the time, Phillip, doing all these cool tricks and thought, *Hell, yes, I'm going to do that,* but many scraped-up knees ,elbows, and falls later, I gave up, thinking, *I don't want to die on this stupid board*—the board cost three-hundred bucks.

Another thing I would do was to go with my family to the gun range. Christmas of seventh grade, my parents bought me a Sig Saur 9mm semi-automatic pistol. It's all black with a fifteen-round magazine. The only reason we got that magazine is that the guy who sold them the gun, John Simpson, was a retired cop, so we got the special one. I was always a good shot and hunted birds and squirrels all the time, eating most of the birds I killed.

This gun was unique—it was my baby and still is. I learned to become a very good shot. I could hit the bull's-eye many times from about fifteen yards away, which isn't an easy thing to do. My dad was about as good as me, but the recoil from the gun hurt his shoulder. Soon after, he bought himself a brand new .40 caliber Sig Sauer (marine or law enforcement edition, I can't remember which), but its silver all over, except for the butt—that's black.

We used to always go to gun shows and look around, but rarely bought anything. I would go to the gun range with my grandpa, too. John always used to sell us the best ammo, Lawman, which has minimum gunpowder spray and doesn't get the gun dirty. We still had to clean it, but it rarely got dirty.

I had grown up shooting BB and pellet rifle guns. I have a .22 long rifle scope that I could use gas-powered rounds instead of gunpowder, which was virtually silent. The first gun I ever bought for myself, I was too young to buy, so my dad bought it, but I repaid him.

I bought a brand new Smith and Wesson .44 magnum, one of the most powerful handguns in the world besides the .50 caliber. As Dirty Harry says, "It will blow your head clean off." One of our favorites of the Dirty Harry trilogy is *Magnum Force*, with corrupt cops and a police director who tried to frame him. As I would watch it, I would see people start to circle around me, so I would think, *Oh God,* and shut my eyes and pray that they would go away.

A crow was always outside perched on my windowsill, crowing at me. To this day, I don't know if it was a hallucination, but it probably was. This was about the time I started seeing demons. I could make out their whole figures—nasty teeth, wings, and small horns coming out of their heads. Some were brown, while others were black—it didn't really matter what color they were. All I knew is something was terribly wrong, but still I kept it to myself.

I would see demons everywhere I went: the mall, movies, or just walking around, even if I was with friends. I thought I was going to hell, because of all of it. I was terrified, but also I would see angelic figures, which made no sense—why was I seeing both? Was I going to heaven or hell? I didn't know. All I knew is that I didn't do anything to deserve to go to hell, so that helped me get past those dark days of my life. It was probably all the horror movies I watched that was putting false images into my head, but I loved them, so I had to make the sacrifice of my sanity to watch them, even though they were bad for a schizoaffective kid.

I suffered from severe migraines, so we went to a neurologist to get checked out. He prescribed me Depakote, which was good for migraines and it was also a mood stabilizer. When I was on it, I was fine, with no mood swings, rage, or deep depression. It should have been an eye-opener, but my mother noticed the difference. I got off it, because one day at my friend's after being in the sun, I passed out. To this day, I think I went through a bout of psychosis, because I remember being in this dream, as if I was in hell. I was screaming to get my old life back and I woke up to my buddy, Dan, shaking me. The look on his face I will never forget—pure terror.

After that bout, his mom gave me two choices: either call my mom or have the paramedics take me to the hospital. I called my mom or perhaps she did, from what I remember. Within fifteen minutes, my parents arrived, which was usually a half-hour trip, they must have been so scared. I was scared myself, but I was so happy to come back to reality and out of that nightmare. I was at Dan's house almost every day after school. On the weekends, we were either at the mall or hanging out at friend's houses.

Brickhouse

MY HALLUCINATIONS WERE STARTING TO GET WORSE IN ninth grade at Brickhouse. I would see wings forming on my teacher's head. Her name was Miss Geanette and I didn't like her one bit—she was too harsh on the students. Ninth grade is also when I met my friend, Shubby, pronounced Shuby. I always loved seeing him get into fights with the teacher. He didn't care what happened to him—he just liked the attention we gave him.

Every Wednesday was Chinese food that we would order from China 1. I would always get sesame chicken with crab rangoon. Brickhouse Academy was a small college prep school of about forty, which I liked because I got good grades without having to worry about hanging with friends. My English teacher, Geanette, would make us read a section of our vocab book and give us twenty vocab words to study and the next day we would have a test. I loved the challenge of it and always got good grades, if I really put my mind to it.

Shubby and I sat next to each other in almost every class. I remember in Spanish class, Shubby had different color permanent markers, so every time the teacher would turn her back, he would mark her white dress—cruel thing to do, but it was funny as hell. Finally one day she caught on and said, "I know one of you is marking my dress," but we weren't snitches, so she never ever found out.

My math teacher, Miss Anna, was my favorite teacher, a beautiful Polish woman with a great personality. Although Shubby at the time had a laser pointer and would shine it on her back, which was hilarious, because she thought we were laughing with her, but we were laughing at her. Finally one day she turned around and he didn't have enough time to put it away, so she took it from him and he never got it back, even after school.

My favorite class was psychology, which was taught by Miss Raymore. She was a widow, whose husband had died of cancer. She was such a nice old lady, so it was in there that we were on our best behavior. It was nice, because sometimes we only had seven students to a class, so I felt more comfortable getting up and giving a speech.

I was still undiagnosed at the time, but I would see that wall open up and a bright light shine through. I wanted to say, "Yes God?" but I knew it was a hallucination. A funny one was when I looked at Shubby and saw that he was white instead of black, which was his natural color. I kind of giggled to myself on that one.

In ninth grade, my parents and I would go to a game room called Livingstons, which I knew all the jackpots and I would earn tons of tickets. I finally saved up enough to get a Rambo hunting knife. I was so excited to get home and throw it at a tree, trying to get it to stick, but I made a stupid mistake with it. I was sharpening a stick to make it into a spear and cut a portion of my finger off. I still have a divot in my finger to this day. I ran inside telling my mom it was pretty nasty and she said "Come on, Steve. I worked in the intensive care unit, I can handle it," which she did and bandaged me up. It was a good story to tell to the friends at Brickhouse.

I've hurt myself a lot in my life. The biggest accident I ever had was when I was in first grade. I was showing off to my friend on the treadmill and got my little toe stuck in the motor and almost cut my toe off—that was another bandage operation for my mother. When I had my Rambo knife and I was talking to my girlfriend and I went to put it back in the holster, it slipped and drove my into my hand, gushing blood. I called for my mom and it probably could have used stitches, but she bandaged it up for me again. When that happened I heard voices saying, "You're going to die from this wound" and "You're a loser, you're never going to get better." I thought it was Satan himself trying to condemn me. I was so scared I just closed my eyes and prayed for it to be over, but it was still just the beginning.

The thing about Brickhouse, Tabernacle, and Lutheran schools was that we had to wear uniforms, which I hated, as we did in the Sarasota Military Academy, which I will get to soon. I was still quite scrawny in ninth grade, but had just almost developed some muscle. I would work as hard as I could every day to where bodybuilding was an obsession. My parents couldn't have been any happier. That was back in the day where I was doing squats that came easy—I couldn't squat much but I loved it.

Same with the bench press, my max at that time was 185. Every time I was done with a set, I would hear a demonic growl in my head, but it sounded like someone was talking directly to me so I didn't know if it was real or not. My dad didn't hear it, so it was just part of my problem. Sometimes I would look in the mirror and not see my reflection—all I saw was the equipment, but not me. This scared me, because I thought I must not be real.

Ninth grade is where my hallucinations started to take a turn for the worse—I was miserable with all that was happening. I started to see black ooze coming from the ceiling and blood running down. When I saw my teacher, she had horns and would make these weird noises. I knew at the time I must be crazy seeing all this stuff. I also couldn't concentrate, even though I tried my best to pay close attention to the chalkboard. But no matter how hard I tried, I would keep seeing these sinister images, noises, or voices. The movie, *The Ring*, came out when I was young. I remember leaving the movie, because it frightened me so much with its images and music, which was bizarre, because I loved scary movies.

We went to see the movie with Tim Allen about Santa Claus where he became Santa. I wanted to go back to *The Ring*, but after that episode, my mom said it was a bad idea. I would sleep over my Aunt Teri and Uncle Mike's house when my cousins came, but I was so afraid of the dark, I couldn't sleep. Even if my cousin was in the bed, I slept on the floor, so I was a sitting duck. My Uncle Mike is a cardiologist and my Aunt Teri is a nurse who helps at my uncle's practice. My Aunt Teri, my cousin Danny, and my mom, and I were watching *The Ring*, so I should have felt safe, but I wasn't. I knew she was going to crawl out of the movie and kill me.

I loved staying the night there before they built their big house, because it was a nice small cozy house, which I felt safe in. I woke up one night out of a deep sleep to see a dark tall man leaning over me. I couldn't even talk, I was so afraid—I just stared back at this stranger in my aunt's house. I closed my eyes and prayed for it to be gone and it worked.

I wondered if it was the work of God or just a lucky draw. I was never very religious, even coming from Christian schools. All I remember hearing them say is, "God put us on this earth as free-spirited people to choose to believe in him—not to be forced to believe in him." That's what I stick to even to this day, but I do believe in a higher power, even though in school they taught us about the Big Bang Theory, which was also plausible. I would only hope there's life after death and I go to heaven where my family is—luckily, not all of them yet.

I remember playing this dolphin game called Echo, which I enjoyed. When we weren't playing that, we would play Resident Evil, which also frightened me, because of the music they would play. Music in horror movies or games set the standard for evilness and that's what scared me.

We used to go to Aunt Teri and Uncle Mike's house for the Fourth of July and shoot off fireworks—mortars that is. It seemed like every time we wanted to shoot them off, it would rain. Maybe it was lucky, so we didn't set anything on fire. We would also go to dinner at a place called Mi Pueblo. I would always get quesadilla, and after our main course, we would have cinnamon sticks to dip into this sauce, which was delicious. They also had the best homemade chips, but I never liked the sauce to dip it in, so I would just eat the chips.

When we would get back to the house, I had a bedtime of 9:30, which I hated, because I was the first to go into the room alone. There my hallucinations got the best of me. I would see the TV turn on by itself and shadow figures come out, but I knew if I went out complaining, I would get in trouble. They would probably say, "Get over it."

In the other room, I could hear them watching the new *Jackass* movie, which I had always wanted to see, but they said I was too young. Hearing them laugh, while they were watching it infuriated me. They didn't have to go to bed at 9:30—only me—and I would sit in the dark hallucinating about everything. Finally when my cousin Brian came into the room, I would feel safer, but still seeing shadow figures and weird faces. Every time I fell asleep, I would have nightmares and every time I was awake, I was hallucinating, so I was in hell basically.

It was worse at the time, because I wasn't used to their house. I didn't feel structured and I just wanted to get home. Sometimes if I couldn't sleep, since my bed was on the ground next to the window, I would stare out at the stars, wishing I were somewhere else like my own home. I would sit there for hours and count sheep. I had a very good imagination, so of course, I would see them, because I was hallucinating. The bed was too hard and the pillow was too sunken in, almost like it was deflated. I would have to sleep on my back, because it was so uncomfortable, and not on my side. I could never get comfortable and when I didn't sleep, it was like World War III. Those were the times my bipolar was at its worst—full of rage and anger, happy, and sad—all at once, I would yell at the top of my lungs, because basically, I was afraid of myself.

When Aunt Teri and Uncle Mike built their mansion behind their old house, which was torn down, it was the most luxurious house I had ever seen. Of the three stories, the second and the third were living quarters, and the first was the garage, in which my Uncle Mike would build or work on cars. He was very talented when it came to cars—he could assemble a car within less than a month. We would get together every Thanksgiving and most holidays. Our favorite thing to do there is have ping-pong tournaments. My cousin, Danny, and my dad are the best at it. They would never stop playing unless we told them to take turns. My dad would always have to work through the pain of his shoulder to play, because it jerked his shoulder too much, because he hadn't gotten the replacement yet.

When I would stay the night, instead of my Aunt Teri letting me sleep in with my cousins, she would make me sleep in a dark office that had a bed for some reason. I was terrified, because I would see these demonic visions crowding around me. I was always so happy for it to be morning and I would wake up to a nice homemade breakfast.

One thing they lacked is a gym, which we had in our back-yard. They have a beautiful house with gorgeous scenery and they live on the water, which was a plus, but I never felt comfortable there—the house was too big for me. We have a big house, but it's one story and sits on three acres. No matter what though, I always feel safe in my own bed.

I loved being home with my family. Every time my mom said, "You're going to Aunt Teri's to spend the night," I knew I was in trouble, because I would have to sleep in that damn haunted office. I would spend as much time with my family as possible and I cherish those memories.

My aunt and uncle had the best walk-in shower—it was huge, and I always wanted to take a shower in there, but never got the chance. On Thanksgiving, they would always have a turkey battle to see who makes the best turkey, either oven-baked or smoker-baked—Uncle Mike did the smoker and Aunt Teri did the oven, but everyone liked Uncle Mike's smoker.

I always remember everyone drinking beer and wanting to drink so bad, but I was too young. My mom and dad would drink, too, but my mom would have a couple cosmopolitans, which is a lot of liquor mixed with juice. My dad would only have a beer, because he was driving, which I admired.

I couldn't watch horror movies there when I slept over, which was probably good, because I would be even more terrified and paranoid in that office—I would always hear noises in there, like growls, music, or talking. Even though I would tell myself that it was not real, I still couldn't get it out of my head. The funny part is that some of the music was soothing, but the other was just scraping sounds, like someone was trying to get in the window, even though I was on the second story. I was so afraid to go to the bathroom, I held it all night. As soon as morning hit, I would run straight to the bathroom to relieve my bladder. My parents would sometimes pick me up early, but mainly later in the afternoon. I was always excited to be home to see my dogs and Grandpa.

My family and I went on my aunt and uncle's sailboat to see the boat show, which was amazing. Bright colors and light music calm my brain enough for me to enjoy the show, while being on the water to me was like opening the first present on Christmas.

I was terrified of the creatures that live in the sea like sharks, jellyfish, and basically everything in the water and I hate when I can't see what's under me to see what is swimming around me. While everyone else would swim, I kept a lookout from the boat. I couldn't believe they would swim in that black water at night— to me it wasn't safe, but I didn't care, because I knew I was safe on the boat. I had a vision when they were in the water. I couldn't see or hear them, but other voices were going on that I ruled out, because my family wouldn't make those kinds of noises or, at least, I hoped not.

I would lay on the boat looking at the stars, trying to find the Big Dipper, which I could only pick out sometimes. I would try to count the stars, even though it was impossible to do. I tried my best to kill time while they were swimming in that cursed ocean. I would look at the ocean at night and it would remind me of my demonic visions. I don't know why, but I think the water at night is evil. The boat show we all went to was majestic and beautiful—bright colorful lights always brought me out of depression.

When we would dock, I knew that I had to stay the night and once again, I was condemned to the haunted office, which I truly thought was haunted, but I knew my visions would clarify that even more for me. Luckily, it was on the second floor, so I felt a bit safer, because I knew unless someone had a ladder, they wouldn't be able to get up to my level. I still never knew why I couldn't just sleep in my cousin's room even on the floor. Maybe my aunt was testing me—I don't know, but I didn't like it, because I could barely ever fall asleep there.

My cousins use to be obsessed with this computer game called Diablo, which was like a futuristic knights game, where you can build up your character and play as him, plus the more points you got the better—kind of like RuneScape, but a lot more sinister. They would play it for hours at a time. I was amazed their computer never shut off. I tried to play it myself, but could never get it right, and I didn't care, since I hated it anyway.

My only obsession was RuneScape, which they hated, but I loved. I would go around asking for girlfriends—not real girlfriends, but game girlfriends. My log-in name was Starling27. I forgot my password, but wouldn't give it out anyway, since someone might try to hack my account. Now I could care less, because I deleted it. I would have a delusion that I was in the game, so no one around me could talk to me, because I was in the world of RuneScape. I would get upset every time I lost a match or my armor. I didn't know how to come back in the world of the living, so I would play it for hours at a time—that's partly what gave me a big belly. Luckily I lost it, but before that, it looked like I had a baby on board. Grandpa Dick and Grandma Dixie were worried for me, because I was getting so heavy, they would tell me I needed to lose weight before something bad happened. A month later, I was back down to my bodyweight, so I deleted RuneScape and never looked back. I was happy to be healthy again and I never picked up another computer game again, even to this day.

My Aunt Teri and Uncle Mike had a cat named Simba, which was like a five grand cat, special-ordered. It was a beautiful cat, kind of small, but nice though. I would always pet it and it would purr its head off. A couple years later, they bought their second cat named Tosh—he was amazing, a huge, special-ordered cat about five grand again. Tosh hated to be touched, so when I would try to pick him up, he would hiss and create a ruckus. Before my Aunt Teri and Uncle Mike moved into their mansion and were still in their old house, my Uncle Mike bought a brand new Ferrari, black with beautiful tires. He took my parents on a little joy ride, but I was too afraid to go for a ride, so everyone got a ride except me.

They would rent out a trailer to people, so they could get a little extra income. It was white with blue shutters, a cozy little trailer. It was only about a mile from their house, which was easy enough to get to, but I never stepped a foot inside, because it reminded me of a horror movie I saw, which looked exactly like their house. My voices were bad enough, so I didn't want to make the situation worse. I knew if I were to step foot into that house, my visions would kick into high gear, so I stayed out. I feel bad, because they wanted me to see it, but I couldn't build up enough courage to do it.

After their mansion was built, my Uncle Mike bought a brand new Corvette, five hundred horsepower. That car flew when he put the pedal to the metal and all my organs shot back, it was so fast. It was all black with black interior and beautiful tires. I wanted to drive it, but didn't know how to drive a manual stick at the time, besides, he would probably not let me drive it anyway. The engine was so loud, my mom said she could hear it from inside the house, even though we were down the street a ways. It's one of those things that you don't pay attention to, at the time you're in the moment and adrenaline is pumping. It was such an exhilarating experience.

Whenever I would stay the night at Aunt Teri's house, my anxiety was full-blown, because everything was so luxurious I was afraid to touch a thing. One day she told me not to hold the stairway bar, because it would get oil on it from my hand. She was very vain about her new house, but I don't blame her. Although it was a bit overboard, I couldn't argue with her, because it was her house.

Some of the scary voices I would hear were saying, "You're never going to leave, you're going to die here." I would just tell myself, "You're all right." I still wasn't diagnosed until later in life, but I will get to that.

When Grandma Dixie was still alive, my mom and I would go Trick or Treating on Halloween. Sometimes I would bring a friend, but it was more of a family thing. My dad usually had to work odd hours, so he could barely come to Trick or Treat, but it was a perfect neighborhood to do it in. I would get a bucket full of candy, but never ate it all.

I remember I was wearing my death costume and I rang the doorbell where this old man came out and screamed back into the house. I heard his wife say, "Oh Harry, settle down." I laughed at that. My Grandma Dixie would give candy out, too, but she would run out of candy so fast—maybe it was because I sneaked a few bits of chocolate.

We always went Trick or Treating in my grandparent's neighborhood, where just a few houses didn't serve candy. Grandma Dixie had a beautiful large mirror in her living room that I used to look at myself every day. When I would take my costume off and went back to the mirror, I would see that my costume was still on me. I ran straight to the couch, frightened as hell, but I played it cool.

After Trick or Treating, I would like to sit in the bathtub. I always made her sit in the bathroom with me, because I was afraid of the drain. I don't know why, but I always thought something was going to come out and get me from it. One day when I was sitting in there, I thought maybe I can do this on my own, so I filled up the tub and got in. I closed my eyes for about ten seconds, but when I opened them, I was sitting in a tub full of blood. It was all over my hands and hair and even when I looked in the mirror, it was still there, so I closed my eyes and prayed. When I opened my eyes, I was back to normal. That was the last time I sat alone in that condemned bathroom—I was a weird kid.

In the bathroom at the beginning of their hallway is where I took a bath, but sometimes I showered. I felt safer showering in the bathroom in Grandma Dixie's bedroom, but once again, she would have to sit in there with me until I was done. She never asked why I wanted her in there, but she always went in with me and kept me safe from the unknown.

I stayed the night there after Halloween and watched the Halloween Scare Fest on SyFy. I would try to get a scare out of myself, but it was impossible, because I was hallucinating day and night. Nothing scared me, except for the dark, which as I mentioned before, meant I always had to have a nightlight.

When I would look at the globe of the world with Grandpa Dick, he would ask me to find things and I always could. We also always looked at maps of Sarasota.

Grandpa Dick is a treasure hunter and a damn good one. He invented this machine called the scanner. I can't tell what it does or how it works, but anything that needs to be found, he finds. When he started to go to Georgia, I would go with him almost every time. The ride was fun, because I could talk to him or watch movies on my portable player. Of course, the movies were horror, but I was in a safe place. My favorite hotel to stay in was Hampton Inn. The beds were so cozy, but not too soft or too hard and the pillow was perfect. His snoring kept me up most of the night, but I didn't care. I just put the pillow over my head and besides, it was cold in there, so I didn't have to sweat all night.

My gramps has always known some of the smartest people— he worked with the government, finding gunpowder and drugs that they would set out. He met a couple of brothers called the Dukes, who worked for the government, also. Derrick Duke was trying to find the Tybee Island bomb. Grandpa Dick set up and "shot" the area to try to find it, but the water was so choppy that his machine, which needs to stay perfectly still, didn't work right and the trip was a bust.

I remember their house on this beautiful lake. They had hot tea as a beverage—twelve cups later, I had to go to the re-stroom every five minutes. I was manic that day, so even before the tea, I had tunnel vision and my whole body felt surreal, like I was floating.

I didn't like to be away from home for a long time, so we would only spend about five days there. We went to this house, but I forget the guy's name. He had wild onions growing on his lot, so Grandpa Dick and I would pick them, put salt on them, and chow down. We probably cleaned out his whole lot, but we didn't want them going to waste. I have great memories going to places like that with Grandpa Dick. I saw many sights and I could actually read the map, knowing where we were and help-ing him with directions, if he couldn't read the map. I knew that made him proud of me.

Before Grandma Dixie died, they would both pick me up from school. Every day, she would say, "Well, did you have a good day at school?" I miss those days, just like I miss my grandma. She and Grandpa Dick were my favorite grandparents. They were both my best friends. Sometimes I still go to my grandma's urn and tell her how much I miss her.

I wish I knew Grandpa John better. I loved Grandma Sharon, but didn't respect her after what she did to my Aunt Teri and my mom. They forgave her, but I never did. Even though she had a bad disease, I still held her accountable for her actions. When I knew her, she had already jumped off the deep end. Alcohol took her from us and made her an evil woman towards my mother.

Grandma Dixie and Grandpa Dick were never drinkers, unless you count some stories he told me about when he was in college. My dad had a perfect life with great parents. I hate when people say they have a rough life and it causes them to drink or do drugs. My mother had a horrible childhood, but was determined to make the best out of it. She got her nurse's aide license at nineteen, then her practical nurse license, and finally, her license as a registered nurse (RN). She stayed an RN for many years and then went on to get a Master's degree to become an Advanced Registered Nurse Practitioner (ARNP). I am so proud of my mom for seeing the light at the end of the darkness.

Back at Brickhouse, I didn't mention my Spanish teacher's name, which Shubby drew all over her back. Her name was Miss Cordovez, a very bright teacher, but also very gullible. She brought us across the street where there was a Spanish bakery and we had to order in Spanish. I would always point to what I wanted, which she didn't know at the time, so I had outsmarted her. However, when I went to try to buy an energy drink, she did not approve.

Brickhouse Academy was on Webber Street in a cubby of a place in a shopping center—very small, but again I felt safe there, because of the small pupil count. The girl at the time that I had a crush on was Erin. She was not too good looking of a girl, but I liked her personality and she listened to the same music I did. We were always just friends though—it never went anywhere. She was a little out there though, as she liked to dress up in Anime attire and go to conventions dressed up as her favorite character. I saw her a couple times, fully dressed up, but never judged her. Even though I wanted to laugh, I didn't, because I had my own problems. I always loved her perfume—it was an amazing vanilla scent, to which I was attracted. I like smells more than looks, but of course, they have to look good, but nothing compares to the smell.

There was a lesbian girl in ninth grade named Tennyson. I can't tell you how many times I said, "Hey, man," or "Hey, dude." She would always call me a jackass and say she's a girl, even though she dressed and looked like a man.

We had a Jewish teacher named Miss Harriot. We would always listen to her speech at Hanukkah and eat some really good potato pancakes. I didn't care what holiday it was—I just wanted more food. I went to the bathroom after all the drinks I had, but when I looked in the mirror, I saw my eyes bleeding and thought, *Now why wouldn't anyone tell me that?* Then it got worse, so I was terrified. When I washed my face, the blood was still there, but when I tried wiping it off with a kleenex, nothing came off. Finally, one more rinse and it was gone, which was very strange, unusual, and frightening. After that, I heard all these screams, so I ran out and everyone was gone. I thought, *Oh God what's happening to me?* I went back in the bathroom and said, "Please, God, make it stop!" I still heard commotion, so I went back out and there everyone was.

This is about the time when I was very close to telling my mom and dad—it was kind of the last straw. I still wasn't on any medicine at this point, but I knew I should have been, but still couldn't tell my parents without them thinking I was crazy.

I had a friend named Andrew, along with Shubby, but everyone thought Andrew was gay from the way he talked. I knew he wasn't gay nor would I judge, because he was such a good friend.

We would make fun of teachers and joke around all day long. He drove a gray Mustang, so I was jealous of him. He asked me if I wanted to drive it, but I said no, because I didn't have a car myself, but he's three years older than me. His parents were realtors, so they had a good amount of money flowing in, but once the market crashed, they lost their house and had to move into a smaller duplex—he even lost his Mustang. He bought a Saturn, which they don't make anymore, and when he lost the Saturn, he bought a Toyota Camry LE—I liked that car.

We would always go out to eat or to the movies. Whenever our food would come, he ordered Pepsi and being at a Chinese restaurant, they had soy sauce, so I would dump soy sauce into his drink. When he drank, he would gag and from there on, the war started. He dumped a whole serving of coleslaw into my Pepsi, which was hilarious. Andrew could always make me laugh. Even in my depressed state, he could still get a laugh out of me. I never told anyone I was depressed, even though I should have. I would sit there stone-faced, not talking and when anyone asked if I was all right, I would always say yes.

We had a Halloween party at Brickhouse, where we could wear everything, but fake blood or a mutilated face. I wore a Ronald Reagan mask, Tennyson a Michael Myers mask, and Shubby a clown mask. Erin wore her outfit and spiked her hair, so Andrew and I would take turns acting like we were putting our fingers in electrical outlets because her hair looked like she got electrocuted. I liked wearing my mask, because no one could see me and I felt safe behind the mask. Obviously, I don't wear masks, but I liked it while it lasted.

We had a teacher named Miss Christina, who was an overweight Polish lady with no sense of humor. Shubby and I were eating lunch. I had a Coke and we were joking back and forth, but when I took a long gulp, he said something so funny that I'll never forget, but I can't say what it was. Anyway, I laughed and cupped my hand so I didn't throw up, but it was too late.

My whole mouthful flew through the air and landed all over her, so she proceeded to call me an animal and threw me out of the class. When I went to the assistant principle and told her what happened, even she laughed, but it was between us. That is one of the best memories I have, but when I came back to class, she still called me an animal. I couldn't stop laughing at it, because although she was wearing a black dress, I could still see the stains.

Mrs. Coleen Brickhouse was the principal at the time and yes, that school was named after her—sweet old lady, soft-spoken—I liked her a lot. The history teacher, Mr. Dillon, was old, chubby, and hacked up a lung every couple of minutes, because he was an avid smoker. I was sitting in his class with a group of kids and I thought it would be funny to sneeze and then said, "Bullshit!" He heard exactly what I said, so off to Mrs. Brickhouse I went. When she asked, "Did you say that, Steven?" I looked right at her and said he might have heard something else, because I didn't say that, she bought it and I went right back to class. He was pissed at me the whole day.

Miss Cordovez took us to this Spanish restaurant on 12th Street and we had to again order in Spanish. I hated that, because I thought, *We are in America, so why should we order in Spanish?* I know it was part of the deal, but I mean, c'mon, really? It was good food though, but Miss Cordovez insisted on eating off my plate. I almost had to bite her hand.

I went to go take a sip of my water, but it was blood red. I knew it was a hallucination, but I couldn't drink it. Being in a clear cup, I know people would tell me if I was mistaken, but that ruined my appetite, especially drinking that contaminated water. On the bus ride back, we rode in a short yellow bus that said Brickhouse Academy on the side of it. We finally got back to school, which I was excited about, even though I didn't like school much. Most kids don't—they just get through it, like I got through it.

Mrs. Wilkes was our biology teacher and I liked her. We went on an outing to this private beach to find specimens of diseased crabs and fish, but we were also allowed to go in the water. Pretty much everyone did, including me, because even though I was terrified of the water, I felt safe knowing I wasn't the only one in it. I found this jelly-filled egg sack and thought it would be funny to hit Shubby with it, so I picked it up and chucked it. Luckily, it wasn't a jellyfish, but I hit him with it and that caused an all-out war with everyone tossing jelly everywhere. Mrs. Wilkes made us all jump into the water and clean off.

The bus ride back was depressing, because the fun was over, but luckily I was dry when Mom picked me up. A couple weeks later, my mom and her friend dropped me off at school, but when I walked to the door, it was smashed. The glass on the out-side sidewalk indicated the perpetrator broke it from the inside to make a clean getaway, since there was an alarm system.

They later found out it was a kid named Patrick, who had gotten suspended from Brickhouse and wanted to retaliate. When I saw the glass, my math teacher, Mrs. Anna, yelled to me, "No school, there was a break-in!" I quickly flagged down my mom who was also in disbelief, but I didn't care—it was a day off school, so I could go home and watch *The Price is Right*. After that, I dedicated my day to watching Stephen King movies like *Cujo*, *The Shining*, *The Mist*, *Pet Cemetery*, *IT*, and *Carrie*.

Then, when my dad came home, I worked out with him. We have the best workouts together, even though he can't bench anymore, because of his shoulder replacement. Even be-fore that, it still killed him, but I always said I would give him my cartilage just to see him happy again—I didn't care what would happen to me. He's the strongest man I know—we both have problems—he doesn't have cartilage in both shoulders and I have a serious mental illness. My mother has nothing wrong with her. I'm extremely lucky to have the family I have that love and support me.

When school was back in session, we all had questions about the break-in, but they wouldn't give us any details, even though we all knew who did it. Patrick didn't make it out with much cash, so prison or jail over something so little is just incomprehensible.

Life at the Brickhouse went on though and classes were back to normal. Our English teacher, Miss Geanette, was back to her crazy self. I remember our receptionist, Karren, bought her a cat sculpture and Miss Geanette flipped out and gave the biggest hiss I have ever heard. Obviously, she loved it, but Andrew and I about died with laughter. She didn't find it too funny, so we got a warning.

We were reading *The Great Gatsby* aloud at the time and went around the class taking turns reading. I liked that book for some reason, and even though it wasn't my type of book, I felt I could follow the story well. I was always an avid reader anyway, reading all my true crime books. Even though I liked watching Stephen King movies, I had still yet to read a book of his, but I didn't want to at the time. I couldn't read my true crime books in there, even to myself, because they said they was too graphic, which was true, but why couldn't I even read it to myself? That was an enigma. Maybe they thought I would go insane from reading them. Little do they know that I actually am somewhat insane already from my mental illness, but all you can do is laugh—right?

I didn't have time to read anyway, because it was a college prep school and they kept us busy as hell. Vocabulary tests every week, essay writings, and other tests consumed most of our time. The thing with Brickhouse is they don't have FCAT, which was a miracle from God. I hated those tests and I don't believe in them anyway. What if you're a bad test taker and have anxiety? Then they put you where they think you belong and it's demeaning to the tester. I think they should have those tests only in college, just to see where you're at in your educational career. They did have other tests in Brickhouse to see if you comprehended your material, but I always passed them with flying colors.

How I was able to manage without any medicine at that time is also an enigma. I made a lot of friends at Brickhouse, but I don't know how. I was a bit social at the time, trying to make friends and forget about my problems which followed, though some days they would lie dormant, while others were complete hell.

My biology teacher, Mrs. Wilkes, was having us play a game on Darwin and we would get candy for every right answer. When she went to the bathroom, I thought it would be funny, so acted like I was stealing candy. When she came in and saw me with a handful of candy, she didn't like that too much, so I was sent to the office once again. It was a fun game, but I ruined it for everyone and she made me say that I did ruin it.

I also met my friend Cameron at Brickhouse. He wanted to be a chef, but I could tell he had tasted one too many cookies, because he was a bit chunky. He was a good friend before he went to culinary school and sometimes he would visit and bring homemade fudge and cookies and truffles. I was still kind of a small kid in Brickhouse—I only weighed 180 pounds and for a 6' 2 kid, that's not much at all.

Shubby found himself a girlfriend there named Nikki, whom he dated for about two years. She was clingy and nuts combined, and he was about twenty-one, while she was only sixteen, so it was not a match made in heaven. I remember numerous fights, with him cursing her out and her firing back—it was such a mess, but he loved her with all his heart.

Then I would hear voices saying I was going to be alone my whole life and that I wasn't good enough for anyone. That upset me, because I thought they were right, but luckily they weren't. I thought if I tried to ignore them, they would go away, but that never happened—it only made it worse. I would hear sinister voices telling me to cut my wrists or jump off the roof or drown myself—just die already. I knew I had to be going insane.

This all happened in the ninth grade and only got worse later on. When I first went to Brickhouse, it was for math tutoring and I think my teacher was named Miss Susan. She was a brilliant math teacher, but not long after I so-called "graduated" her class, she was arrested for check fraud.

I loved Miss Karen, the receptionist. She was funny, sweet, and caring all in one. When she left Brickhouse, I was deeply upset, but didn't know what I could do about it, so I just let go.

One day, Andrew, Shubby, and I were in Miss Geanette's class and she went to draw an island on the board, but it looked just like a penis. Andrew and I about died laughing our butts off. The whole class joined in, so we were sent to the couch in the front part of the school to hear our fate from Mrs. Brickhouse. She was such a nice lady, so we got off without being in trouble.

When we got back to Miss Geanette's class, she was writing on the board. It looked to me like the letters started to come off the board and float around her head, so I kind of snickered at it, but when she turned around, it was gone. I thought it was a bit funny, though I kind of just learned to try to make the best of it.

I recalled the time Shubby and Miss Geanette got into it over his lunch and words were flying. Finally Shubby goes, "What are you gonna do, hit me?" She said, "I wouldn't do that, Shubby." Then she basically ran to get the principal. we all died laughing, because she was walking so fast, her hair was blowing backwards. She couldn't prove it, because the whole class denied it, since nobody liked her at all—she was so demanding we couldn't take it.

When Miss Geanette came back into the room, she turned off the lights and made us sit and think about it. We didn't care at all, because we knew we were free from work that day. We just sat until the next class, so it basically was not a punishment, but a gift. I just put my head down and tried to sleep. If someone woke me up, I was going to say that I was praying. I learned that trick from a friend. That would only exasperate the situation, so I never said that to her.

I would get paranoid, because while I was sitting in class, I would hear my named being called out. I would turn around and think, *Where the hell is that coming from?* I never found out, so I knew it was a hallucination.

Mr. Dillon the history teacher was horrible. He didn't even teach, but would pick out an exercise in a book and made us read and write what it was about, while he would go out and have a cigarette. I will never forget the smell when he walked back into the room. I felt like saying, "Get some Fabreze, man." Then he would sit there and hack up a lung, which made me feel bad, because he acted like it hurt like hell. But an hour later, while I was in another class, I would see him walk by on his way to have another smoke, because my class was right next to the back door that he would walk out. It's weird how not all smokers smell when they're done with their cigarettes. Some smell the same as they did last time they smoked, but Mr. Dillon was a different story. He could fumigate the whole room with that stale scent.

The best part is Shubby and I had all the same classes and we would sit next to one another and joke around. But when it came to schoolwork, I tried to be on my best behavior, because I knew that high school was extremely important—the college you wanted to go to lay in the fate of high school.

In ninth grade, I had my dream set of wanting to become an FBI profiler. I thought I would be good interrogating witnesses, talking to criminals, and getting inside their heads. I would have to be very manipulative, which I can be when I want to be. I don't believe in the good cop/bad cop routine—I believe in getting information any way I can. If I had to take the gloves off, I would. Sometimes you have to be hard on these lifelong criminals to get the feedback you want. Everyone at Brickhouse thought I could do it and be good at it. They knew I had the smarts to achieve my goal.

I loved Brickhouse, because on Christmas, we had three

weeks off instead of two. That was a plus for our school, which I called the Little Academy.

I didn't have a girlfriend, but didn't want one at the time, because I knew my hallucinations would get in the way. If I got stressed, that would be a living hell for me, so I steered clear. I had girls as friends, but never in a relationship. It was easy for me so I didn't have to go through the whole breakup routine with the crying, and the cursing, and saying, "Well, I cheated on you anyway" bullcrap. Of course, I was instantly attracted to any pretty girl and always thought, *Man, if only*. But I remembered what I told myself and kept away, but man, was it hard to do!

The only girl at the time I was attracted to was Erin, and what attracted me was her vanilla smell. I loved it and told her so, but in the end, we were only friends, which worked out perfectly. Even Tennyson had a huge crush on me, because she was bisexual. That was pretty nasty, but I was nice to her and so kept her respect. She was nice and all, but I had no attraction to her and I didn't like her smell. There were pretty much no girls in the school, since we only had forty students. The only one I liked was Erin, but like I said, we were just friends, but *not* friends with benefits.

Being a freshman in high school, I felt that I needed to set the standard high. High school is some of the most important years and I wanted to make a good impression. Even though I joked around a lot, my grades never slipped. Miss Geanette would give us a spelling and vocabulary test every week. She would give us a couple days to study up, so I would make flash cards with the word on front and definition on the back. I would either ace the test or get a B, for which I was proud of myself.

Sometimes my parents and I would go to JoTos Japanese Steakhouse, either for good grades or my birthday, and I've been going there ever since Tabernacle. I would get the JoTos triple special with lobster, swordfish, tuna, squid, or shrimp. The appetizer was a soup with salad and they would also cook rice and zucchini, and they prepared everything right in front of you. One of my favorites were the mushrooms—I would eat every single bite and some off my dad's plate, because he hated mushrooms. I must have consumed over two thousand calories there, but it was all worth it in the end.

Back at Brickhouse, we had a snack shop, which consisted of Pop Tarts, chips, and drinks—it was pretty cheap, but it was delicious. I usually got a strawberry Pop Tart with a Coke and sometimes a bag of Famous Amos cookies. I kept asking when they were going to include energy drinks, but they told me never in a million years. I was half-joking, but I decided to ask, because it never hurts to ask. I would just bring my own in and watch Miss Geanette as she watched me drink it, knowing or at least thinking I was going to bounce off the walls.

With my mania, the caffeine would actually calm me down for some reason. I didn't know it was mania at the time, of course—all I knew is I felt great. It's as if I wasn't in my body, but I was floating with no pain or emotions, except euphoria, and no one could stop me. I was a working machine and prayed for it never to go away, but I knew there was going to be a deep depression that followed that would drag me to hell.

When I was in that state of mind, I could do my homework in ten minutes literally and read a two-hundred-page book in forty minutes. I felt like a genius, because my mind never stopped and I was enjoying every bit of it. I never understood how mania works or what the effect is on the brain, but I didn't have to do drugs to feel it—all I had to do is wait for it to come.

About two weeks later, my whole world dropped—horrible depression, pessimistic thoughts, thoughts of suicide, but never thoughts of homicide though, thank God. I was fifteen at the time, so I couldn't drive to school, but I didn't care, because I didn't have to worry about hallucinations popping out in front of the car. When I did, while my mom was driving, and I knew she didn't see them or she would try to dodge them. Riding to school, I would see people standing on the top of light poles, stop signs, yield signs, and power lines. They were following me everywhere I went and I couldn't shake the feeling of paranoia and guilt for not telling my family. I wasn't put on medicine until I was out of high school, but I will get to that later. For now, I had to suffer the consequences and the anxiety.

Every day I'd think, *Life would have be better, if I would of just open my mouth and say something*, but I was afraid. Whenever I would stay home from school, it wasn't because I was sick—it was that I was having a bad day with hallucinations or depression. Mania meant that I didn't care, because I could do anything I wanted, but the anger part of my bipolarity was starting to brew. I remember cursing out Tennyson for no reason at all. I made her cry, but then later, I went back and apologized. It's all part of those damn mood swings. I didn't care what people thought of me, but I knew to make it through ninth grade, I had to pretend that I did care about what people thought of me.

This was the first time I saw my amazing social worker, Scott—he helped me through so much, I'm in his debt. Unfortunately, he died of cancer, but I knew him for about six years before he passed, which was a very upsetting moment. The last time I saw him was when he needed my truck and me to help move one of his patients into an Assisted Living Facility, which I gladly accepted. He introduced me to my favorite book of all time, *An Unquiet Mind* by Kay Redfield Jamison. I must have read that book ten times in my life. It's very inspirational and I can relate to her, even though she's not schizoaffective like me, but she did go through some psychosis—just not nearly as bad as mine. One day when I was reading her book, the letters again started to fly off the page, making a black paper with the words floating on it wrap around my head. I yelled, "Stop it!" I was alone in the house, which is the reason I yelled, so I closed my book and didn't read the rest of the day.

I've had a lot of scary visuals. One of them is where I was sitting in my room and everything started to rot around me—the walls, my TV, my bed, and my computer all stared to decay. Soon I was sitting in an empty room, wondering when it was going to stop. It happened again one day at school, when everything started to disappear, so I put my head down and asked, "Please God, make it stop." This is the time you'd better believe there is a higher power than that of man.

Later that day, I went to the bathroom and turned the light on. Then I went to toilet and when I was done urinating, I looked in the mirror and saw black ooze coming from my eyes, so I quickly washed my hands and face. When I opened my eyes again, it was gone, so I rushed back to class where I felt safe. I guess my face was pale, because everyone asked if I was all right. I felt like saying no, but I said yes. I just wanted to be left alone at the time, so I excused myself from class and sat on the comfortable couch in the front office area. I just told them I had a migraine, which I did at the time, so I wasn't lying. While I was sitting out there, I was looking out the window and the phone rang. Karen picked it up and was talking, but when I turned around, she wasn't on the phone anymore. I was still hearing it, so I called home and left early, telling my mom I was throwing up.

Grandpa Dick picked me up, because after Grandma Dixie died, he moved in with us. I missed going to his old house, but was happy he moved in with us. Every time I called home because I was sick, he was right there to pick me up. He even picked me up every day at school, because my parents were working. He never complained once, even though I'm sure he was happy when I could drive.

I was fifteen, so he didn't have much longer to have to pick me up before I had a car, which was pretty much freedom in my book. However, I was afraid of driving, because I knew my visuals were going to interfere with my driving skills. When I received my restricted license, I would try to drive everywhere my parents let me. Yes, I was seeing hallucinations, but I tried to forget about them. When I would see the roads flooded, I would slow down, acting like I was trying to concentrate on the road, but it was tough.

I would also drive my grandpa's car, which was fun. My dad had a truck, which later became my truck—I loved it—GMC Z71 2005. I just didn't know how to park it correctly, because it was so big and it was a gas guzzler, something like sixteen miles to the gallon. My mom had a 2006 Camry LE sports package with BBS rims. It was a beautiful car, which again became my car, but I had it before I got my dad's. Her car dove well, had a nice engine, and the ladies liked it, so that was a big plus, but I could only sit and wait until my birthday. I would have auditory hallucinations telling me if I drove, I'd die and that I'd never amount to anything, even if I did drive. That was depressing, because I thought they were true statements.

I saw all my older friends driving and having a blast. Sometimes Shubby would pick me up and take me to school and come back over and work out. I liked working out with my dad the most—he's a big inspiration to my friends and me. I always wished I could be as big as my dad. His highest bench press was a whopping 425, but I could believe it, because he is so damn big.

This is the time I started losing hope, while I was having all these problems. It's hard to focus and do the best you can, when you're having hallucinations and depression. My parents thought I was only depressed—not having hallucinations. It wasn't fair to them, not knowing exactly what I had at the time and I still feel guilty to this day for not letting them in on my big secret. It felt as if I didn't have any friends—even though I had a lot, I always felt alone. Sometimes I liked that, because some friends can let you down and I didn't want that to happen. Some friends can also get in the way of your future, meaning they can stress you out to where you can let your grades slip away into failing and that wasn't an option for me. In ninth grade, I had Shubby and

Andrew as my good friends and that's it. Even when I would see Erin, she wasn't a friend, but more of an acquaintance, like many others there. I would always see my parents talking to someone, but they didn't call them friends—they only had a few friends, too, like me.

My friend, Andrew, had a soft voice, so many thought he was homosexual, but I knew he wasn't. Even if he were, I wouldn't care, because he was a good friend. He also picked me up a couple times from my house to drive me to school and back to my house. I liked his driving, because he was a defensive driver. Shubby, on the other hand, was a crazy driver—we had many close calls, but I still wasn't scared for some reason. I thought, *Oh, well, it won't hurt*, nor did I care at the time—I just wanted to be put out of my misery.

We would always go to the mall, which I liked, but I still didn't want to be anywhere but home. I thought with a crowded mall, maybe my hallucinations would go away, but I was wrong. It's hard to tell what's a hallucination and what's not, but when I saw little goblins running around, I thought, *Okay it's not Halloween, so this is fake. It's not real, so just get a hold of yourself, Steve.*

I kept strong and stayed with my friends. At the time, I think I was with Shubby, but he was always fighting with Nikki on the phone. It just wasn't fun to be around with him like that—lots of F-bombs being thrown around. Then the crying would come and the apologies flowed like a waterfall. The next time I saw him out of school to hang out, the same damn thing happened, the fights and the breakups and back together was like clockwork. Andrew had just gotten out of a relationship with his girlfriend at the time, but the good part was he never called her while we were hanging out and he showed no emotion towards it.

Shubby would take on any dare. We were having Chinese one night and I dared him to eat five raw oysters and, of course, he did, but there was no money involved—just who had the bigger gonads and I turned out the loser with the tiny gonads. They had crawfish and I remember they started dancing right in from of me, jumping off the table, and just dancing away—I laughed so hard at it. I couldn't help it and I know damn well the whole restaurant was thinking I was insane. The funny part is that I am, but they didn't need to know nor would I care. It felt like the movie *Flubber* with Robin Williams having things dance off the table—I couldn't help but laugh.

When Andrew and I went out to eat Chinese, I learned to order water or a clear liquid to make sure he didn't put soy sauce in my drink, but he never learned, I would always pour the whole bottle into his Pepsi. Shubby and Andrew would have to drive since I was too young, so I would buy most of their meals— cheaper than gas at the time.

When Andrew and I would meet at Friendly's, we had a fa-vorite waitress named Mary. We loved pissing her off, or at least Andrew did, especially the time he put coleslaw in my drink. There was no hiding that, but it was funny as hell. It seemed like every time we went to Friendly's, we always got Mary and I know she was thinking, *Great, those bastards again*, but what could we do? We were hungry boys. Andrew may have gotten a little something special from the cook, but not me, because I was always nice and polite and left her a good tip. When Friendly's used to be around, that was Andrew's and my favorite spot to eat. I overheard Mary talking about Andrew and when he put coleslaw into my drink, she said, "Little bastard never learns." I never told him that, because I hate drama, so I kept it to my-self. He wouldn't have said a thing anyway. Mary was an older lady, maybe in her sixties, with large thick glasses. She had half-dark and half-gray hair. She was nice and respectful, except to Andrew. It was my job to keep her calm and relaxed, or she might have killed Andrew.

I was living a lie—not even to my best friend could I say what I was going through or they would tell my parents. Getting me help before hurting myself and getting me the help I needed, I rejected that thought because in my head, if I were to go to a mental institute, I was afraid I would never get out. They would only do it for my best interest—never to hurt or just to send me away. I knew it would happen though, and then I would have to see the look on my parents' faces, which would have been devastating. I felt like I had let my family down. I didn't drink or do drugs, so why did this have to happen to me? I was a good kid, always polite and respectful, and a shy kid, so why was I stricken with this disease? I didn't know the answer to all of it or any of it.

Sarasota Military Academy

MY DREAM SCHOOL WAS SARASOTA MILITARY ACADEMY (SMA). After ninth grade, I switched over to SMA for tenth grade—I liked the military structure and discipline they instilled into us. Every morning, we would stand in our uniform, pledge to the flag, and hear some military sayings while saluting the flag. I was happy knowing so many people cared about our country. We wore red berets, a green shirt that said Sarasota Military Academy, and green wool pants that were itchy as hell. We also had to wear name tags displaying our last names only—no first names allowed, because that's what they do in the military.

I didn't mind—I loved every bit of it. We had to tuck our uniform in, which I hated, because I never tuck in my shirts—ever—and the uniform was hot, so I hated going outside. My whole body would sweat and it always showed through, especially under my armpits, so I would try to stay in the shade.

Lunchtime was around noon and we could go anywhere on campus to eat, but I always ate with a group of friends. Tenth grade was tough being in a new school, especially with new faces and new structure. It was very strict, but that kept my hallucinations somewhat contained, because I was staying busy and doing all my work on time.

Random drug tests were administered throughout the campus. Many kids failed and had to go to an alternative school like Triad, which no one wanted to go to. Luckily, I never did drugs, so when I was picked, I passed with flying colors.

Lots of good-looking girls were there, but they couldn't wear makeup, so when you saw their true beauty, just imagine what they looked like with makeup. The men had to have a crew cut and ladies had to have their hair up and not laying on their uniform—weird rules but no one complained. Jewelry was not permitted. Tattoos could not be shown, so if someone had arm tattoos, they would have to wear the SMA jacket—if it still showed, you couldn't attend the Sarasota Military Academy. I didn't have any tattoos at the time, so I was good to go.

A couple days into tenth grade, I saw my best friend, James, who I hadn't seen all ninth grade and we hit it off again. However, he was a truant and missed more days than he was there. He was put on probation at the time, meaning if he missed anymore school they would kick him out. The days were fun with James. We made lots of videos of us goofing off and other funny antics.

One day I'll never forget is when we were pledging to the flag and all I saw were skeletons—everyone was all bones. It stayed like that for quite a while and I didn't know what to do at the time, but I kept strong and pulled through it.

I liked the reading class—our instructor's name was Captain Salhany. He was a nice guy with a deep New York accent, which I would joke about with him. He make us read and write an essay of what we read, which I thought was a brilliant idea, so no one cheated, because they had to read all of it to get the story or essay correct. We could read any book we wanted, as long as we wrote another essay about it, but I didn't care—at least it was a book of our liking. He was very impressed with my writing, but I had to give credit to Brickhouse for that from all the writing and vocabulary words they made us do there. My thoughts always shot off in different directions but if I really focused, I could write one hell of a paper. Everyone respected Captain Salhany, who gave his students many chances to ace his class.

We had a female instructor, also, but I forget her name. All she would do is play Solitaire on the computer, but she never got up once. She made Captain Salhany do all the work, and thought she was being sneaky, but I caught her playing it. She didn't know that if I want to find something out, I will.

Still to this day, I have this hallucination where the room fills with floating black clouds and it starts lightning and I hear thunder. Then it would rain, while all I was doing was sitting at the table. I must have looked out of it, because this girl named Valerie shook my body and I snapped out of it. I always thought someone would report me, thinking I was on drugs of some sort. The teachers would have had to know, because I looked dazed, but they never said anything. If they did, they could drug test me, which I didn't care about.

I just didn't want to give the wrong impression, especially to Captain Salhany. He was such a laid-back teacher, but I do remember him asking me after class one day, if I was all right. I said, "Yes, I'm just a little tired is all." I know he knew something was wrong, because I never purposely dozed off in class, but if I did, that meant I was having visual or auditory hallucinations. I remember the voices saying Captain Salhany was a fat slob and he's going to kill me—evil voices like that, but I just ignored them, no matter how loud they became. It was extremely hard to concentrate when all that was going on, but I tried to focus on him and his voice only.

After being in Brickhouse for ninth grade, I wasn't used to such a large class. I felt very uncomfortable, but all I had to tell myself is that I would make lots of friends. At this time I was still reading true crime books, which were very graphic, so he didn't like my book reports on it. However, he let it slide, because I was at least reading a college-level book, which no one else was reading in his class.

I learned from Brickhouse how to read such a sophisticated book. I had always wished Shubby were there with me, but I know damn well he would have been expelled. The poor guy wouldn't last one day before being kicked out and then he would be right back to Brickhouse Academy or, if Brickhouse didn't allow him back, to Triad.

Since Captain Salhany was one of my favorite teachers, I never goofed off in his class. Even if I had a friend in there, I still wouldn't have goofed off—no one disrespected him while I was in his class.

A new girl named Sia came to Captain Salhany's class and asked me to show her around the campus after class. I helped her with her work as much as I could. Her first assignment was to read an essay and write about it. I basically told her exactly what to write down and she was a good listener, so she aced the essay. Since I was new, too, I didn't know the campus either, so while we were in class, I tried to remember the campus that I did know from walking around at lunch. She was a beautiful girl with brunette hair, slim body, and exquisite breasts and she smelled good, which attracted me, also.

Before class was over, when I was supposed to show her around, I had a visual that everyone in the class was bald, with blood all over their heads, so I excused myself from class. I went to the nurse complaining of a headache and she let me go home. The next day, when Sia asked what happened to me showing her around, I said I had gotten sick. I was helping her with a crossword puzzle that the class were working on at the time. We finished first, because it was good teamwork. We didn't win a prize, but we did win bragging rights, which is basically the same thing in my book.

Captain Salhany came up to me once asking about James, since he knew we were best friends. He asked if he was always hyper and if he ever did his work. I said just to be patient with him and respect him when he did a good deed like his work. I told James myself to respect Captain Salhany and it worked. He aced his test and was able to read the book of his choice like the rest of the class.

That was one of the few times he was ever at school. If he liked SMA as much as he said he did, then I don't know why he stayed away from school so much. In a way, I understood, because he had a very sick dad, who had had multiple strokes. He was looking out for him, so I didn't blame him, but in a way, school is more important. I would want to make my dad proud of me by going to school and making the best of it.

Even Captain Salhany knew something was wrong. He would always ask me where James was and I always told him he was sick, but wasn't sure how long I could keep lying about it for. Unfortunately, James and I never had any classes together. I know I would have been able to help if we did—I may even have saved his high school career, but I had no control over it. Captain Salhany was the first class of the day, so after morning pledge was his class. We would have to stand still and salute, making sure we didn't lock our knees. I probably saw three people a day pass out—some had seizures and the paramedics were called to check them out, but they were back to normal within forty-five minutes. By the time I got to his class, I was soaked with sweat. I was so embarrassed, but then I found out we could wear white undershirts, which I did and that problem was solved, thank God.

Every damn day I went through class hearing auditory hallucinations. I would hear voices saying I'm a failure or that everyone hates me. I would hear whispers in my ear and then I would see colors, either red or blue, but no other colors. I would ask Captain Salhany to go to the bathroom and sit in front of the mirror saying, "It'll be okay." Then I would wash my face and remember looking up to see this evil-looking lady behind me. When I turned around, she lunged at me, so I ducked as fast as I could and she missed me. When I closed my eyes, she was gone.

I ran back to class after that and was always afraid to use the bathroom ever since. I would make sure there was someone else in the bathroom with me. I must have been as white as a ghost, because the captain pulled me aside. I was sweating, so he asked if I was okay. I said, "Yes, I am, thanks for asking, Captain Salhany."

I would try not to drink water, so I didn't have to go to the bathroom, but I knew I had to drink, so it was a sacrifice to myself. I would put a wedge in the door to keep it open a little bit. However, it was a big bathroom, so there were many places things could hide and come out and get me. I tried to make it safe and then run back to Captain Salhany's class.

I went home "sick" again from bad visuals the day I was supposed to walk Sia around campus, but the next day at class, I promised her I would take her around, so I did. I walked with her on the bricks that we stood on in the morning and then I took her to the cafeteria, the offices, and watched people play Hacky Sack before we ate lunch together. I also went to the gymnasium to play basketball, but all we did is shoot hoops. At the end of it all, I deserved a kiss and I got one.

I was sixteen at the time, and had freshly passed my driver's test in my mom's car, but I still didn't have a car. I couldn't take my parents' cars, because they were both working. My mom would drop me off at school and Grandpa Dick would pick me up afterwards. I didn't care, because out of school, I could drive my mom's car anywhere I wanted.

I forget my curfew time, but it was like eleven or so. I didn't plan on staying out that late anyway, since I had to get home to sleep. While I would sleep, my friends would be at parties, but I was never the party type. I knew if I didn't get sleep, it would be hell the next day. Also, I didn't drink or do drugs, so I wouldn't have fit in anyway. I was a very shy, quiet boy, but not so much after I was diagnosed. I would try to make friends as much as possible, and succeeded.

My friends, Brandon, Max, and I, would eat lunch together, even though we didn't have classes together. I forgot how I met them, but they were good friends of mine. Through them, I met lots of other people—not my friends, but it was nice being around people. Sometimes we would eat in the cafeteria to get out of the sun, which was like heaven sitting in the cool air conditioning. We would swap lunches, if we liked each other's food, and get either a Pepsi or a yogurt. I would always get Brandon's sour cream and onion chips, which were my favorite. It was only a week into school and I already knew all these people—I loved every bit of it.

The next day was Captain Salhany's class. Sia and I were holding hands under the desk, trying not to get caught. We would hold hands all class, even when trying to write an essay or anything—we were glued together. I thought it was a bit odd how we were already connected in such a little bit of time— literally a week—I liked her though and she liked me. Captain Salhany must have seen us holding hands, but I don't think he cared one little bit, because he knew he would do the same thing. Whenever he would turn away, we would sneak a kiss before he turned back around. Those were good memories that I will cherish forever, because she was so beautiful and she picked me to like out of the whole school. That's only one of the moments I will cherish for life.

While I was with Captain Salhany, James was in weightlifting with Coach Collis, an arrogant asshole, pardon my language, but I will get to him soon after my classes. I would always say everyone is a genius in some way—you just have to find it. I loved that saying and carried it with me everywhere I went. Whenever I would have a problem I would recite that to myself and know I could do the task at hand.

The one and only thing I hated about Captain Salhany's class was even though we were a week into school, he had already started to go over FCAT prep. I was thinking, holy Christ, already? After a full year of Brickhouse, where we didn't have the test, I wasn't ready for FCAT. Now I had to learn everything there was about it. The reading and writing came natural to me, thanks to Captain Salhany, and he made sure no one failed the reading portion. After Brickhouse, my vocabulary was great from all the tests we would take, plus it was a college prep school, so I knew a lot of words. I could write a two-page front and back essay within forty minutes—probably not the best time in the world, but I knew it would suffice. The best part there was that I barely had any corrections. I would always spell my words correctly, which was thanks again to Captain Salhany and Brickhouse.

Tenth grade is where I picked up my first Stephen King novel, *Cujo*, which was easy to read. I could write a report on what I liked and from there on, I was hooked on the book. I aced my essay about the book and I read Stephen King almost every day. *Cujo* was easy for me to read, even though it was a sophisticated book meant for adults, not tenth graders.

I'm always up for a challenge. I didn't care if they gave me a dictionary to read, I would read it and give a five-thousand word essay about vocabulary words. Luckily, that never happened, because that would be a bit difficult, but I don't care—throw that ball and I'll hit it in the sweet spot.

I also think I got my book reading skills in sixth grade when Mrs. Timmons gave us a book called, *A Short History of Nearly Everything*, by Bill Bryson, a college-level book for sixth graders. It was such a fascinating book, I wish I still had it, because I would read it over and over. Too bad I didn't have it in Captain Salhany's class to read—I would have given the best damn book report ever—still it was pretty difficult to read.

I have a memory of a delusion I once had. I was an informant for the FBI and they were trying to contact me for a special mission. I could hear them talking inside my head, saying I needed to contact them to accept. I typed a long letter on the computer saying that I would accept the mission and that they wouldn't be disappointed in me. After that letter, I kind of popped back into reality, but the letter was already sent, so I couldn't take it back. Luckily, they didn't break down my door, saying we got a delusional kid here—take him away. And, of course, then came the paranoia, thinking the cops or the FBI were going to come in and frame me and take me away to jail for a long time. Then I would have a record and wouldn't be able to work anywhere, because people don't accept felons to work at their place of business.

Then I thought, why would this ever happen? I've never even had a speeding ticket before, so why would they be after me? I just had to talk myself down. I also thought Captain Salhany worked for the FBI. I was on special alert about him, but I kept quiet. Obviously, he didn't, but in my state of mind, I thought anything was possible.

Not too long after that, we were all standing at attention and I saw four unmarked helicopters fly by. I was looking directly at them, but no one else was. I thought, *Why the hell does anyone not care about what's going on?* When they opened the door and started firing, I jumped back. My friend goes, "What the hell is the matter?"

I said, "Don't you see the helicopters?" I'll never forget his face. He looked at me concerned and sincere and asked, "Why don't you go see the nurse?"

I said, "No, I'm fine," and went on with my day. Luckily, he didn't tell the nurse or I would most likely have been drug-tested. When they found out I wasn't on drugs, then what? I couldn't tell anyone, because I was afraid I would be locked away in the loony bin, if I did.

My friend, Nolan, is the one who asked me to go to the nurse. I could tell he was scared for me, but I never gave in. Nolan also told James, who was my good friend, too, and then James was scared for me. Nolan asked if I was doing mushrooms and at the time, I didn't know what that meant, so I said, "No I'm not on any drugs at all." I was sort of pissed for them thinking that. When I found out what mushrooms were, I had wished I had done them, because at least after a couple hours, I would be back to normal, but I wasn't. I had a severe problem and didn't know how to address it at the time.

My bipolar was pretty bad at SMA. I would have rage and euphoria all at once and I couldn't channel my anger correctly, so I would blow up on people, but somehow never got into a fight. To be honest, everybody was afraid of me, but I don't know why. Maybe I was having a delusion of people being afraid of me, but I was a ticking time bomb.

I would rather be bipolar than schizophrenic—I've heard some of the smartest people are bipolar. My idol, John Nash, was a great mathematician, but had schizophrenia. I always thought, *I wish I could be as successful as John Nash*, but he was worse off, because he didn't take medicine. The funny part is, neither did I in tenth grade.

Once while Captain Salhany was teaching, I heard a British accent saying the captain was going to be murdered within forty-eight hours. I thought it was my mission to keep him safe, but I couldn't do a thing, because it was all in my head. The voices were being projected like someone was talking to me in real time. The difference with me is that I feel like they are right there talking to me. I felt like I didn't belong anywhere at the time, like a ghost, because no one could hear me complain—not that I was going to complain anyway, but I felt alone.

My parents were always there for me, but like an idiot, I still kept quiet. It would break their hearts, if I told them what I was seeing, hearing, and feeling. I feared no one at this point, because I thought, *If I'm going through all of this, what else is there to fear?* At least, you can hit back a real person, but not a visual, but my visuals were getting worse as the days passed.

I also had horrible stage fright. Captain Salhany was always trying to get me to read one of my essays in class, but I just couldn't. I didn't know how to start, and my hands would shake and my sense of hearing diminished. I felt like Helen Keller, because sometimes I would get blurry vision, so I had no sense of hearing and little eyesight after about five minutes. When I sat down, everything would turn back to normal. I don't even remember how I got back to my seat. I must have glided there, because no one said anything to me about a single thing.

After I was done reading *Cujo* in Captain Salhany's class, I picked my favorite book, *An Unquiet Mind*, by Kay Redfield Jamison. I wrote the best essay about it. I received a first in class for writing the essay. I still read the book today, because it's so inspirational and gives me insight every time I read it.

I was continually hearing a cacophony of voices at the time and didn't know how to work around it, but amazingly I did. At the time, I was going through psychosis, but I didn't know anything about it at the time. The weird creatures, helicopters, voices, and the delusions were just the start to being in a living hell. I missed Brickhouse, because there I could walk out of class and sit on the couch to cool off. At Sarasota Military Academy, it was either class or the nurse. I sometimes chose the nurse and then after I calmed down, I'd go back to class—my excuse was a migraine. Even in the nurse's office, I was hallucinating. The paper on the wall would drip down like rainfall and the nurse had pins sticking out of her head like the movie, *Hell Raiser*. I kind of snickered at that and the nurse goes, "Well, since things are so funny, go back to class," so I did, but that image still made me chuckle to myself. Whenever Captain Salhany asked about the nurse, I would always say, "Oh, it's just a headache, I'll be fine." His accent always made my day better. Instead of saying, "car," he would say, "caw," or "yawd," instead of "yard."

Sia also knew something was wrong, but I don't know how. I mean, I thought I was acting normal, but must not have been. She would ask if I was all right and I would say, "Yes, hon, I'm okay." She liked being called, "hon." We never dated, even though we were attracted to each other. I was just not ready for a relationship at the time, because I knew stress meant more problems. After a while, I was ready to date, but not that time.

Man, was she attractive though, especially when she curled her hair and wore Victoria's Secret perfume. While we would talk,

I would hear voices saying, "She's poison," or "She is a whore," or "It will be a toxic relationship." However, I never dated her, so I didn't care, but those were harsh words to say to such a sweet innocent girl such as herself.

I would also hear voices saying Captain Salhany was a fat degenerate slob. He was heavy, but not a slob and he was a very caring man. Now the teacher who would play Solitaire *was* a slob for never helping him out when he needed her. Whenever he would ask her a question, she would reply saying, "I don't know," without even researching it. She was a waste of space. I didn't have any respect for her.

It was impossible to get a low grade in his class, because he taught it so well and everyone loved him. I even told the colonel at the time how much I liked him and that he needed a raise.

My friends from childhood, Taylor and Brad, were there, too, and they were high in rank, but I was just a basic with nothing but my nametag. I didn't care about rank—I wasn't there for that—I was there for education. I didn't have any plans to join the army nor could I. With my hallucinations, that would be an accident waiting to happen. I would never put another's life in jeopardy, ever.

I was standing at ease, which means you can stop saluting and stand with your hands at your side relaxed, when I saw everyone turn into robots and begin yelling at the top of their lungs. I couldn't make the words out, but I quickly ran to the bathroom, which I could have gotten in big trouble for doing, but I didn't care—I just wanted to get the hell out of there. I looked into the mirror and saw a lady staring back at me with black eyes. I wasn't safe, because anywhere I went, my visuals kept following me. I washed my face again and cautiously went back out, but everything was back to normal. I thought I was possessed by a demon—that was the only logical explanation, so I believed it.

I thought, *If I was a demon, why don't I have powers like invincibility or reading people's minds?* At one point, I thought I could, but it was just my voices. I thought students were talking to me through mind power.

I remember in Captain Salhany's class, I thought people could read my thoughts, so I tried not to think. Of course, it was a delusion, but I still tried to refrain from thinking. I thought it was a gift from God, who gave me the ability to read thoughts, predict the future, and control people through mind power. I also thought I was telekinetic and could move objects around with my mind whenever I wanted.

I would have visuals, where I thought I was moving something and thought, *Hell, yes, I did it!* If only I could move that lazy teacher off her ass from playing the stupid Solitaire card game. I don't even know why she had a job there—she never got up except to make copies of whatever she was doing. She would leave the room to go to the office, where they had a copy printer machine. Sometimes she never even came back—God only knows what the hell she was doing. Probably out smoking a cigarette, because I swear I smelled it on her.

She had an easy lazy laidback job, watching him teach while playing on the computer. I wish I would have unplugged it, but she probably would have had a heart attack with no working computer, or just go find another one, but oh no, her Solitaire game would not have been saved—that's the real heart attack right there. I want to say her name was Miss Dracket, but that was my math teacher, while I was attending Brookside Middle School. I didn't even want to ask her name, because she sickened me. I didn't like the way she looked, even though it was mandatory to wear uniforms tucked in.

The wool pants were so itchy, I was constantly scratching my legs. Especially when my legs were sweaty, the pants stuck to my body like glue. Wearing those clothes in the morning when the sun was high and hot, I would be drenched with sweat and my uniform would stick to me, even after wearing one of those berets on the top of my head, sweat would trickle down onto my face. No matter how badly it itched or how much sweat was coming off my head, I had to stand perfectly still, but I never did. I would wipe as much as I wanted to just to get the sweat to stop from running down my face. After wearing the berets, when I took mine off, it was soaked, but I didn't care—it wasn't my problem—I went to class drenched. Poor Captain Salhany probably smelled a thousand different smells of people's sweat. All the teachers stood in back of everyone in the shade, which seemed unfair at the time.

Unlucky kids were dropping like flies waiting in line. Even though people knew not to lock their knees, they did it anyway.. The whole reciting and parade rest, or at ease was fine, but we stood at attention for close to 20 minutes at a time. It may have been a ploy just to get out of morning pledges, but they would actually pass out. Some had seizures and there was one poor soul who had an ambulance check him out—respirations, lungs, heart, blood pressure, and temperature—all that good stuff was almost all were back to normal the same day.

One day, Captain Salhany pulled me aside and said, "You're not like other students." That was a compliment, but he also saw a side I didn't want anyone to see. He said, "Steve, there is something wrong here. I see the way you look at things as if you've never seen them before and you look out of it in my class, but still get amazing grades. Is anything wrong with you?"

I just looked at him and said, "Nothing at all, sir." I was afraid of getting expelled, which they would have never done, but it's just the way I thought. A lot of the time in his class, I would hear loud music playing across the hallway. I go, "Man, that's some loud music, huh, Captain Salhany?"

He goes, "What music?"

I said, "Across the hall."

He asked me to go into the hall with him, so I did. When we got out there, he says, "Steve, there is no music at all."

Standing in the hallway with him, I realized it was gone. I

was so embarrassed that I asked if I could stand in the hall for a minute, but he said to come back in fifteen minutes. He could have easily asked to drug-test me, but he kept quiet. That's what I loved about him, and also that he was very laidback. Even James liked Captain Salhany, which was incredible, and he also got good grades in there with him, which is one of the times he was actually at school. The rest of the time, he was helping his dad with his older brother, Peter. He also had three sisters, Annabel, Jessica and Helen, and a half-sister, Emilia. James is also an uncle.

The days he came, we would goof around at lunch and when Captain Salhany would walk by, we would say, "Did you pawk your caw in the yawed?" He would always laugh at that, because he knew we were kidding. We made sure not to overkill it, so we only joked every once in a while.

After Captain Salhany's class, we had Self Defense, which was a fun class. Our teacher was a guy named Soke, a big black fat guy with abs that would kill you if you ran into him, but he knew his stuff. He did a form for us and remembered every bit of it. His partner, who we all called Sensei, was a skinny black guy— weird mix, but they were great instructors.

I had already been in martial arts, so I had the jump on everyone. I could still do splits and they were very impressed by that. He would teach us how to punch, kick, and dodge strikes and jujitsu. It was one of the best classes I ever took. Every strike we threw, we would have to say, "Uss," no matter how funny it sounded. I got caught not saying it once and had to do one hundred pushups, which sucked.

All our parents signed a waver saying we might get hurt and asking for their permission to put his hands on us, and all the parents signed it. We would stand in three separate lines and Soke would walk around punching everyone in the stomach—he didn't hit lightly either. The girls got a soft one, but on the other hand, the boys got a whopper right in the breadbox, which he meant to do and we would keel over in pain. Every chance I had to show off, I would ask for another punch, but even if I had to clench my abs tight, it still felt like a car rammed into my stomach. I don't understand how he could be so obese, but his abs protruded through his shirt. He gave me a free punch once and I nearly broke my hand on his stomach. It was like hitting a steel pole.

The first time I ever saw an angel, I was in Soke's class, sitting down while he demonstrated a form. I looked over and saw an angel—not just any angel—it was beautiful, but had black wings looking up at the sky. I knew at that point, it was a fallen angel or a demon trying to get back to heaven, but God didn't allow it. At first I thought, *That's what I've been hallucinating, a demon trying to get back to heaven*, but then I stopped and told myself it was only a dream that would be over soon. Then the roof came off in the gymnasium and the angel flew into the sky, so again I ran to the bathroom to wash my eyes and tell myself to keep it together. When I went out, everyone asked if I was okay. I must have been white as a ghost again.

After forms, we would see who could kick the highest. I always won, because of my karate background—not even Sensei could kick that high. I think he was jealous of me, because he could not see how this little kid beat him. At the time, my friend, Thomas, would always antagonize Soke, asking to be punched in the belly. I'm amazed he never got hurt or threw up—he was a freak of nature. I would volunteer to be punched in front of our class of around twenty people. He always hit me right in the breadbox, which was probably what he was aiming for, to be honest. After about twenty gasps for air, I was fine and, of course, I wanted to do it again to show off, but never antagonized him like Thomas did.

One day after I got out of the bathroom, I went to join the class. When I walked out, balloons were everywhere—on the ground, in the air, and on the stage, so I went back into the bathroom and thought, *Okay, Steve, here we go again with the hallucinations.*

I walked out again and they were still there, so I went with it. When I tried to kick one balloon, my foot ran right through it, so I knew it was a one hundred percent hallucination. I went back into the bathroom once again, washed my face, said a little prayer, and it was over—thank God.

Although I'd rather see that, than demons, monsters, or discombobulated and mutilated people. I would also see people hanging off the ceiling, but I was in class and couldn't do a thing about it, no matter what I did. I knew I wasn't safe anywhere. Behind closed doors, in the bathroom, or walking around, they would follow me everywhere. Some people with schizoaffective see happy things. I wish I were one of them, but all I saw was evil and ominous figures. The only happy one was all the balloons of different colors I saw in Soke's class.

Soke's abs were so swollen that I could see the outline of every muscle in his stomach. He must have weighed over 350 pounds, but he could still move extremely fast, which I didn't understand how the hell he did it.

The best part is there were a lot of pretty girls in there, including Sia, but we were just friends. I never asked her out for some reason—maybe I was afraid of the drama that might have happened and would make my hallucinations worse. I didn't understand how they could get any worse than what I was already going through, so I just stayed strong and Soke helped me through his whole class.

This hallucination made me laugh and I saw a monk wearing his robe kneeling and praying. I thought, man, if only I had visuals like this instead of evil ones. He just sat there and prayed, so I kind of looked around to see if everyone saw what I was seeing, but of course they were oblivious. I had to make the best of it, so I laughed and my friend, Will, looked at me with a concerned look, knowing something was going on.

James has Self Defense after I did and he would get kicked out for mouthing off, so I knew he got a few punches to the breadbox. I went to go use the water fountain and when I turned it on, nothing but blood flowed out and I never ever used that fountain again. Although I knew what it was, it just didn't satisfy me enough even to take a sip.

We didn't work out or do Self Defense in our uniforms. We would change into shorts and a sweat-proof T-shirt that I loved, because it wasn't our itchy wool pants, but we did have to tuck them in. It was a pain in the ass after being all sweaty to change back into our uniforms. It would always stick to my body, which was very uncomfortable.

One day I was looking at myself in the mirror flexing, of course, and I saw blood trickling down my chin. When I opened my mouth, it was full of blood, so I rinsed it out. I was missing a tooth, so once again I washed my face and looked back up and it was back to normal. It looked so real, I swear I could taste the iron taste of blood. I had that taste the rest of Soke's class.

I was the only one in the class with a martial arts background, besides a kid named Saul, who was amazing at jujitsu. I was pretty good myself, but I was no comparison to Saul. My punches and kicks were harder and more accurate than his, so I wasn't too worried about it and he was a nice kid who wouldn't hurt a fly. He knew enough moves to defend himself, but that's about it. I was still a small kid at the time, being 6'2 and 180 or 190 pounds. That's not very large, but maybe if I were just a bit shorter, that would be a huge kid. I did have a good set of abs though—a perfect six pack. I also had great veins that would protrude out—I loved having veins like that.

Soke showed us a video when he was early in his martial arts career, knocking a guy out with a head kick in ten seconds. It was incredible to see it and gave me even more respect for Soke. I didn't like Sensei, even though he also was a good teacher and good at martial arts. I though he was an arrogant man, who tried to show off as much as he could. He was a very skinny black man who thought he was God. The funny part is, he probably weighed as much as me at the time, but he looked emaciated. Every Thursday was physical training, with stations set up for pushups, crunches, bear crawl, medicine ball training, and running around the gym. He would push us to our limits, which was a very entertaining experience.

I was hearing voices the whole time, to the point where I saw my partner's lips moving, but couldn't hear him. I know he was getting frustrated, because he probably thought I was ignoring him, but I wasn't. The voices were getting the best of me.

I can't say what my voices were saying about Soke or Sensei, but it wasn't nice words, I'll tell you that much. I loved every bit of Soke's class. Besides having to change, the uniform was already sweaty from standing outside to pledge, so even taking the clothes off was a battle. Putting them back on was like trying to put them on soaking wet, plus, they were cold from the sweat of sitting in the cool air conditioning.

They gave us Sarasota Military Academy black jackets, which I always wore, because I didn't tuck my shirt in if I was wearing it. It could have been 100 degrees and I would still wear my jacket—that's how much I hated tucking in my damn shirt. My uniform shirt was already too big for me, because I had a thick neck and they measured by that because we had to button up every single button, so finally we found one my neck would fit into, but it was extremely baggy and would puff out if I didn't have on my jacket. The only problem was that after Soke's class, I was extremely hot, but still wore my jacket—it's amazing I never passed out from heat.

Soke would always tell us never to use what we learned in his class on other people in the school. If we did, we would get a couple punches to the breadbox. It was rare for him to kick someone out of his class. James was the only one he ever kicked out that I know of. If he ever heard James making fun of him, he would give him a couple punches to the breadbox.

Whenever I was having a bad day, I would ask Soke to allow me to sit out the class. When I had to do it, I enjoyed it, but I didn't tell him I was hallucinating, even though I was. I was seeing tall grass that was covering everyone and I could only see the tops of their heads, so I put my hand out and started to push the grass aside as I was going through. I know people saw me doing it, but it was the only way I could see them.

While in Soke's class, I was going through a deep bout of depression. Nothing satisfied me or made me happy—not even being around my friends. I had to put on a fake mask that I was happy. I liked Soke's class so much, because the discipline he bestowed upon us was the best and it sometimes made me happy knowing I was going to his class.

I remember sitting in class on the stage getting ready to go through our routine, when I saw a severed head rolling towards me, calling me a prick over and over. I tried to ignore it, but it wouldn't go away, so I complained of a headache and went to the nurse's office. I called Grandpa Dick to come get me from school, which he did. That severed head will be in my memory for life—how real it looked and sounded was terrifying. There wasn't any blood though, which I probably would have smelled, but maybe not.

Every day in Soke's class, he would put the twenty of us into three lines. We would stand there as he walked around punching people in the stomach. I clenched tight when he hit me, but it's amazing I never lost my bowels. We watched a Bruce Lee movie and he would make us practice what we saw which was impossible, because Bruce Lee was too sophisticated for us, we didn't have the mind set or power to even come close to him.

Tenth grade was tough for me, because that's when my schizoaffective started to develop rapidly. I had no warning—it just got worst, because in ninth grade, it first showed its ugly face. By tenth grade, it started to spread through my entire brain.

My anger was starting to worsen, too. I was able to hold it back or else I would have gotten into many fights. Knowing how strong I was and with my temper, I would have hurt someone. I just remember what Soke would say, "Channel your anger and frustration for better use. That use will come to you one day, if anything bad were to happen." I remembered that saying and never got into one fight at school, even if they were provoking me. I kept my cool and remembered Soke, who pulled me aside one day and said I was his best student. That touched my heart, because out of probably one hundred people he saw every day, he picked me. I tried my best to make him proud, but not as proud as I tried to make my parents of me.

I can't think of anyone who upset Soke besides James, because everyone had respect for him, but not as much respect as I had for him. I always looked forward to his class, so I didn't even care about my uniform after a while. The gym shorts and shirt we had to wear for any physical activity were very comfortable, but physical training outside in our uniforms was brutal. I don't know why we didn't wear our gym shorts and shirts out there. I would come back absolutely soaked with sweat, and I can't imagine what I smelled like, even though I always wore deodorant and cologne. As always, I was wearing my jacket, so I didn't have to tuck in my shirt.

I was never caught, probably because they didn't care, as long as it wasn't showing. Even though I was wearing an undershirt, I still had sweat stains showing, which was very embarrassing. Armpit stains were the worst, because it would start to itch and I couldn't stand there scratching—people would think that was gross.

Every Friday in Soke's class was grappling day. We would do wrestling and jujitsu, trying to submit our opponent in any way possible. Lucky for me, I was also a good wrestler, even though I didn't have any experience, but I would submit everyone I could. The only time I was submitted was by my friend, Joe. He got me in a rear naked choke, which is where you wrap your arms around your opponent's neck and lock it in with your other hand to cut off the blood supply to the brain. You have no choice, but to submit or pass out. I could have held on longer, because I had a massive neck, but I know it would still cut off my carotid artery. It doesn't matter how strong the neck is—as soon as you cut that artery off, even if you're still breathing, the lack of blood will make you pass out.

That was the first and last time I was ever submitted, not to sound like I'm a god, but I knew what I was going and I was damn good at it. I used armbars, leg locks, rear naked chokes, heel locks, and kimoras. While I was grappling, and this happened a lot, I would see my parents cheering me on and giving me thumbs up. I would hear laughter and claps, which only made me work harder at what I was doing. At the time I thought it was real, but then realized, *Why the hell would my parents be there and no one else's parents?* As I looked around, I didn't see anyone clapping, so I just tried to ignore it, although it was difficult. As I looked around, I could see black ooze falling again from the ceiling and running down the white paint in the gymnasium.

Some days, Soke would surprise us by putting the grappling mats on a Tuesday or Thursday, as well as Friday. We all loved grappling, but luckily, no one ever got hurt, because then our class would be canceled and that would be a big bummer. Grappling is what everyone there looked forward to in Soke's class.

My tenth grade experience was anything but perfect. I tried to hang in there for my family's sake, because I don't give up. I'm not a quitter, but some days were far worse than others. Soke taught me self-respect and to love myself for who I am. If I ever told him what I was going through, I bet he would've said, "Don't let it take control of your life." I'm sure Soke probably thought something was wrong with me, the way I would stare off into space, sometimes talk to myself, and have that blank stare on my face with no expression on my face—just a stone-cold look.

Soke's lips were moving, but another voice was coming out, like a childish voice—I couldn't make sense of it, so I just went along with it. Bad part is, what if it was important? How would I be able to hear his real voice, instead of some foreign voice?

I called home many times and sometimes, I would go home, but at other times, my mom or dad would say, "Tough it out— school is very important." I couldn't ask Grandpa Dick, because he would always say yes and then, I would miss so much school, I'd be backed up with homework.

There was no homework in Soke's class, besides practicing forms and our punches and kicks. Soke made us stretch out before we started, so we didn't pull anything and to get head kicks. A leg kick to the body or head are the most important, because it generates so much power in one single blow.

I always had a voice in my head saying, "You can take Soke on, you got this—just murder him—you can do it." I knew if I ever did, I would be killed by a punch to the jugular. I remember grappling Sensei once. He was extremely easy to catch with an arm bar. I tapped him out twice, one with an arm bar and the other by guillotine, which is another type of a choke blocking off blood to the brain.

In Self Defense, I met this beautiful girl named Demi—at least to me, she was beautiful—I didn't care what anyone else thought. I would practice my forms with her, teach her the proper stretches, and just hang out with her on down-time. We would chitchat about anything and everything. She was blonde, a little overweight, maybe ten pounds over, which isn't bad—I liked the way she was. She always had her hair up and looked very attractive, even though she was forced to have it off her collar. She had the best smelling perfume that I was attached and attracted to. Even her lotion smelled terrific. I think it was Bath and Body Works lotion and perfume that she got from the mall.

A voice in my head said she was poison, it wouldn't work out, and I had to leave her right away. It wasn't just in my head—it felt

like someone was saying that in my ear, which was even more dis-
turbing. We weren't even going out at the time, so maybe it was a
sign that I never listened to, but I was sure mistaken. Whenever
we would do our forms in class, I couldn't help but stare at her
butt. It was so nice and she also had perfect breasts. I didn't have
any other classes with her besides Self Defense. I was happy with
that because I didn't want to get tired of seeing her. This way
we were always excited to see each other without thinking, *Oh
Christ, there he (or she) is again.* I always liked to show off in
front of her, especially at grappling on Fridays. I was submitting
everyone I came in contact with. I wasn't big at all in tenth grade,
but somehow I was as strong as an ox. I didn't have a single bit of
fat on my body. I was a machine that plowed through anybody
that got in my way—not too many people wanted to grapple me
after seeing me submit everyone. Soke was very impressed with
me and would keep me after school sometimes to teach me a few
more things that I didn't know, which I respected so much.

One day he was in front of me teaching and I was in back
following his lead, when I saw a millipede crawling up his leg.
I was about to say something, but he didn't seem to feel it—he
definitely would have felt that big of an insect.

I laughed at him one day, because when he turned around, he
was white with a black man's facial features—no other part of his
body was black. He looked at me like I was crazy, but I just said
I had a tickle in my throat.

Not too long after that in Soke's class, I was waiting for a
good time to ask Demi out to be my girlfriend. So I asked her
at lunchtime, which she accepted, and we went steady. I couldn't
take her on dates, because I didn't have a car and I wasn't about
to have my mom drive when I took Demi on a date.

Finally my prayers were answered—I can't remember if it was
for my birthday or Christmas—Uncle Mike hit me with a big
surprise. He gave me a lone key and brought me outside, where
right in front of me was a 1995 GMC green three-seat truck,

manual transmission. I had no clue how to drive a stick, so my dad took me to deserted parking lots and taught me how to handle it. I caught on in about a week, so after I learned correctly, I never grinded the gears.

I was going down the road near my house, probably going about 45, with a biker right next to me. I was thinking, *Damn, this guy is fast,* but when I reached the light, he kept going right into traffic. I honked my horn at him, but when he got into traffic, he vanished, so I thought I'd better get home and relax. I couldn't drive like that, since I wasn't used to them at the time, but I soon learned how to tell the difference.

When I got the truck, I felt free—I could go anywhere I wanted, but only if I told my parents and they approved. I was finally able to drive to school by myself. SMA has a parking lot for juniors, but only the seniors parked on campus. Since I was a sophomore, I had to finesse a little bit, but was finally able to park in the junior lot.

My truck was a tank—nice body, very heavy v8, and held about 21 gallons of gas, but it was also a gas-guzzler. I had some problems with it, but I still loved it—I just didn't want to have it break down on me in the middle of the interstate or a busy road. I've never told anyone this, but one day I was walking to my truck and my truck transformed into a giant robot like in the movie, *Transformers*. I didn't know what to do at the time, because I was in the SMA junior lot, so I couldn't drive like that nor was my truck a vehicle anymore—it was a robot. I know people were watching me in a weird way, because I was just standing there with a blank look on my face. I just waited about twenty minutes, walked back up to school. I saw Soke, so I visited with him a bit. When I went back out, my truck was there—I was so relieved.

The brakes on the truck weren't too good, so I would have to slow down considerably to make a clean stop and the tires barely had any tread, but I drove as much as I could. Sometimes my mom would let me borrow her Camry LE sports package, and it later became my car, but I will get to that. Some days when I had my truck, I would pick up my friend, Nolan, and we would drive to Albertsons, get a gallon jug of sweet tea, and then head to school. I loved driving my truck, because this is before my truck started to let loose a little bit. It had good pickup and I like driving fast cars, but that would eat up gas even more rapidly than before.

Even though you could fit three passengers in it, I only drove with two at a time. Otherwise, I would have to reach between someone's legs to shift gears—that was a bit weird in my opinion. My shifter went into the ground, instead of being on the steering wheel, which made it easier to shift. I had always told myself I wouldn't drive a manual, but now that I knew how, it was fun to shift gears.

I was driving to school alone one day to pick up Nolan, but on the way there, I heard a whisper. When I looked beside me, I saw a woman maybe in her forties with blonde bloody hair and a bloody face saying, "Help me, please help me!" I was so happy when Nolan got into the truck, because I was scared and just wanted company. I was lucky to have a two-seater, because then I didn't have to worry about someone being behind me in the back seat.

Demi was finally able to get into the truck with me, but she lived fifteen miles away, so I never picked her up or dropped her off. I was being lazy, plus, the wear and tear on the truck wouldn't be healthy for it, because I didn't know if my truck was on its last leg or not. Some Saturdays I would drive to her house and visit with her, but never brought her back to my house, but later after high school she did once. Demi had a jealous ex-boyfriend, Garrett, who hated me probably because I stole his girl. The funny part is that we had math together, and he would threaten me, but I didn't care. I knew I could tear him a new ass. I was worried about him knowing what my truck was and where I parked it, because he was the type of kid that would trash a car, because he was afraid to face me. That never happened, because I secretly drove off every day after school.

Some days, when I was late for school, I would have to park in a different lot. If the parking lot monitor told me I couldn't park there and there wasn't anywhere else to park, I just went home. I had a free day from school, but I didn't complain, because I was happy. I would go home and see Grandpa Dick. Grandpa Dick and I spent a lot of time together. I would take him for rides in my truck, but I couldn't gun it or go fast, because it would make him nervous. On the days I didn't go to school, we would watch *The Price is Right*, just like I did with Grandma Dixie. He would also take me into his shed to show me his latest invention. Sometimes he would let me use his metal detector around the yard to see what I could find, but I found nothing really of interest.

Some days when I had nothing to do, either because I had finished my work ahead of time or it was a fun day, I would try to sneak out of school. The monitor made sure no one sneaked out. Somehow, I found ways to get past him, but it was a waiting game. This was during lunch, but as soon as he left, I would run out before he got back and sneak home.

I brought James once and we went back to his house. I felt like a secret agent on a covert operation. We went to Babe Ruth baseball field and played catch and Home Run Derby to see who could hit the farthest. Those were some of the best memories of my life, but I have many more memories. We would always use wooden baseball bats, because aluminum bats are too easy. The wooden bats were somewhat cheap and that was good, because we went through two a day each, taking turns on who bought the next one.

James was an amazing baseball player, who wanted to play for the Yankees, but never got that far, because of some of the choices he made. He played his whole life through and was top of his class at Cal Ripken baseball fields and the same with Babe Ruth fields. He hit many home runs in his day and never lost that talent. I never liked to be pitched to, because I was afraid of being hit, but he talked me into it and, of course, where did the ball go? Landed on my left shoulder, which caused the rage to build up and then came the yelling, cursing, and sweating. I wasn't on medicine at this point, so I just had to try to cool down myself and tell myself he didn't mean to—at least I hoped not, but I could have killed him, I was so infuriated. We never did that again, just threw the ball in the air and hit it with no pitcher. I was seventeen at the time.

Back to Demi, I started not to like her as much as I did before. Not only was I not as attracted toward her, I was also getting tired of Garrett bitching at me every day, so I broke it off with her. That was the biggest mess I've ever been through. The crying, the telling me I'm a loser—I was having voices at the time, so all I heard every day was noise. All during lunch, she was begging and crying in front of the whole school. This lasted for about a week, until she finally understood it was over. I had many girls ask me if I was beating her. They believed me when I said that I wasn't hitting her or anything.

That was one of the most ridiculous ordeals I've ever endured. As she walked away, I saw a little dwarf flick her off, so I laughed, which didn't help the situation. Even after telling me how horrible Garrett was, she went right back to him. She was probably trying to get back at me, but I didn't care, because at least she was off my back for the time being. Demi told Garrett I hit her, so I had to deal with him saying he's going to kick my ass, but I wasn't afraid—as I said, I would tear that kid apart. Then he said, "Fine, I'll crack you open with a baseball bat," but I would have loved to see him try, because if I got ahold of the bat, it would be game over for little Garrett. He wasn't little, though he was very overweight. Demi tried to flirt with me a little to get a rise out of him and it worked, but he would complain to her, not me, because he knew it wasn't me that time.

He had a lot of friends that could have easily jumped me and gotten away with it, so I was always on guard to look out for them and I was already paranoid so that didn't help at all, but I was comfortable with my martial arts skills, so I wasn't too afraid. I sat with some friends of my own and I knew they would have had my back if it came to it. The ironic thing is that our math teacher's name is Captain Garrett, a beautiful woman about twenty-nine years old—she was also a soccer coach. When Demi's boyfriend, Garrett, sat in front of me, he would turn around every once and a while to stare me down. Finally, one day in class, I go, "Why don't you take a picture, faggot? He didn't know what to do or say at the time, because I said it in front of the whole class of maybe fifteen people.

Before math when we were in Soke's class, I met my best friend, Tyler, who is basically my brother now, We would always joke around with each other. We would practice our techniques together and help each other stretch before class. On Thursdays, when we had our physical training (PT), we would always be partners.

The first day I met him when we were partners, he had black eyes with black ooze running down his cheeks, but I ignored it as much as I could. We just hit it off and about a week later, we were and still are best friends, but we're brothers now.

We also had weightlifting together with Coach Collis, the prick I brought up earlier. Once again, Tyler and I were partners, helping do bench presses, curls, and dead lifts. After I saw that I knew he would be a great workout partner and having a gym in my backyard, I invited him over to work out. He picked me up from school once day and was going to drive me home. That's when I was introduced to heavy screamo metal—I have loved it ever since.

I'll never forget the look on his face when we entered my gym—it was amazing. He goes, "I thought you had some weights with a Bowflex or something, but this is like heaven." At the time, we could lift the same amount of weight and both of us had great cardio. After I knew him for a while, he invited me over to have a UFC night that I usually had at my house, but I'll get to that. Anyway, it was Brock Lesnar vs. Cain Velasquez and it was Tyler, his friend, Cohen, and I all watching it and we were let down when Brock lost. Tyler and I also went to the Sarasota Boxing Club together. I was good at it and amazing at the speed bag, and he was an incredible boxer who had been training for many years at Absolute Boxing. I had enough friends at SMA to keep me moving and motivated.

In weightlifting class, Tyler and I were the strongest kids there and we were almost as strong as Coach Collis. He was a very rude man and anyone who tried to correct him on his form was sent out until class was over. I know this, because I told him how to bench correctly. While benching, we had to put a rolled up towel on our chest—not that it would do any good if you dropped the bar with 225 pounds on your chest.

I was sent out one day into the hallway, when I was upstairs for my class. I saw a man standing about fifteen feet away with a noose around his neck. He turned to me and said, "I'm sorry for the troubles," and he jumped off, breaking his neck. I knew it was a hallucination, so I didn't pay any mind to it. I didn't want to be there any longer though, so I persuaded Coach Collis to let me back in, if I promised to work hard. I always worked hard, but it was never enough for him. I don't remember Tyler ever being sent out, but maybe he did, because we worked out our own way—not what Coach Collis taught us, but what my dad taught me and I taught Tyler.

My hallucinations were starting to take a turn for the worst. They were happening closer and closer together, so sometimes I didn't know what was real from what was not. I always felt safe around Tyler though, but never told him my secret either. Tyler and I were working out at my house one day and messing around with water bottles. I had my shirt off and so did he, but he thought it would be funny to pour ice cold water on me. I flipped out: my body got red, my pupils were as big as saucers, and I went on a rampage punching the metal machines and cursing. Finally I snapped out of it and told Tyler I was sorry for doing that. I knew from that point on, something was wrong—a normal person would never freak out like that from such a benign incident. I should never acted like that, because he's my brother. I would never do that to him, if something weren't wrong. Luckily, it wasn't in Coach Collis' class or I would have scared everyone, including Collis.

While working out in his class, I would hear evil voices saying, "Enjoy it, you're going to die tomorrow. You got nothing in this world, you're going to burn in hell with us," and other scary voices like that saying evil things. I didn't know how to stop it, but I didn't want to be sent away forever from my family and friends.

I used to host a UFC Fight Night at my house. I would invite all my friends over, if they paid a small fee like ten bucks a person: Tyler, Cohen, Joe, Shubby, Dylan, and David, and other good friend that I'll get to. We all had so much fun—they would all stay the night in my room, which somehow we all fit.

After the fights, I thought it would be a good time to watch *The Fourth Kind*. Shubby was very into voodoo, since he was Haitian, but the movie scared him so much, he stood all night without moving, didn't sit or lie down, literally stood all night. We would scratch the walls or growl, but at the time, it was funny, but I can't imagine what poor Shubby was going through. I was used to scary movies and even that movie scared me! They tried to make it look like a true story, but of course, it wasn't. It was all fiction, which I tried to tell Shubby, but that didn't work.

I have a lot of amazing memories with Tyler. His parents are great, too—they're like my second family. The first time I ever went over to his place, they gave me a nice hug and introduced themselves. Tyler and I were always getting into mischief. I remember the pond in his backyard was empty or almost empty, so we took his truck and jumped that pond many times. I even shot a video of it, which vanished.

We used to have bonfires every time I slept over there. We would always put gas on it and create a gas trail, which was my idea, so when we lit it, the fire would create a perfect trail leading straight to the pit. He has a tent that we would use sometimes when we camped out in his backyard, until we heard noises that scared us back inside. If Tyler knew the voices I was hearing, his ass would be inside in two seconds. I swear I saw a yeti once, sneaking around the tent. It still scares me to this day—the way it looked and the sounds it made were horrific. All I could think about is it getting into the tent as it was ripping us apart. I didn't tell Tyler, because he would have freaked out even more. He wasn't a wimp, but we can't really defend ourselves in the dark and dead of night.

Tyler and I would always go to the mall either Friday or Saturday, when it was busy. We would try to meet new people and talk about others as they walked by. Spencer's was our favorite store, with lots of gag jokes and items, and f.y.e., where they sold movies and music. Perry's BBQ is a Chinese restaurant with the best orange chicken around all Sarasota. The Sarasota Square Mall was only about ten minutes from his house and after the mall, I would sleep over. We didn't go to sleep right away, because we would watch movies. *Day Breakers* was my favorite movie about vampires, where the whole world were vampires with a few humans and blood was running short. Then we would watch some *Family Guy* or *South Park*. We finally fell asleep with the light on.

I was glad it was on, because when I opened my eyes, I was staring right into the eyes of the devil. An ugly creature with black eyes was five feet away from me. I about had a heart attack, but I didn't want to shut my eyes, because if it was going to kill me, I wanted to be ready for the pain. It must have been five minutes, but felt like five hours, before it finally disappeared. I didn't sleep anymore after that ordeal. I turned on *Family Guy* and watched it for the rest of the night, while Tyler was still dead asleep.

I was so close to telling him what I saw, but I didn't want him telling my family, while trying to look out for my best interest. I told Tyler I must need anger management, since my mood would switch from nice to evil. I never thought in a million years that I would be schizoaffective, which is bipolar and schizophrenia combined, but it gives me a better insight of the world.

Soon Tyler was coming over almost every day and we would work out and play *Call of Duty: Black Ops*. Tyler would get so caught in the game that every time he died, he would use profanity and jump up and down. At the time, I had Xbox Live, so we were playing live people—that was the best part, but it was a tough game. I would see the players coming out of the TV after me, like I was watching a 3D movie. I didn't like that, so I would go into the bathroom, wash my face, and come back out. If it was still happening, I would ask to watch a movie and soon it got better.

Tyler wasn't a dummy, so I was sure he knew something was wrong, but he never asked except once when we were going to 711, because I wanted pre-workout pills. I couldn't get them, since I was only seventeen, but when he said no, my whole attitude changed. I turned into an evil monster, yelling and screaming and cursing all at once. It made him cry, because I was being so damn mean, but finally we hugged and I apologized and that was it.

Tyler was going to anger management, because he also had a temper, but never to me, because we were brothers and never fought. Sometimes, we just had arguments that neither of us ever won, because we both made good valid points. His room was full of posters that I was always jealous of, because they looked amazing: posters of rock bands, women, and funny drinking posters. His bed was one of the most comfortable beds I've ever slept in besides mine. He liked scary movies, too, just not the gory type. I was fine with that, because some of the scariest movie aren't blood and guts—the suspense is what keeps it going.

Tyler was with us when we watched *The Fourth Kind* with Shubby, but I felt bad, because he was so superstitious. At the time, Tyler worked for his dad, who owned a lawn business. I don't know how they could work in the sun all day, but they did. The night before we watched *The Sixth Sense*, I was home while he was working and went to the kitchen to get something to drink. When I turned around, I saw a lady in a pink robe, who said, "Help me, Steve, help me!" Her wrists were cut like in the movie, so I didn't get a drink, but I went out to Grandpa Dick's room and spent some time in there with him. While I was sitting there, the lady in pink passed by into my room. I thought, *I'm never going in there for the rest of my life.*

I brought my dogs everywhere I went, because I knew they would keep me safe. If they didn't growl or bark, I knew it was safe. I wasn't afraid of the movie *The Ring*. Tyler and I watched it and I think it scared him, because at the slightest noise, he would turn around and say, "Did you hear that?" I agreed with him that it was the blinds. I never brought up noises that I heard, because I knew for a fact they weren't real. The hallucinations were starting to get worse, but the more I tried to hide my problem, the worse it got, because I wasn't venting to anyone. Even when I would stay at Tyler's house, I would see shadow people circling around the bed, which made me feel very unsafe, so I scooted to the middle of the bed. He would complain that he didn't have any room, but I felt safe closer to him.

Even though Tyler and I had Soke's class together, we never grappled nor did I ever want to risk hurting my best friend. By the time I met Tyler, my truck had been sold, because it had more problems than not, but I had my mom's Camry LE sports edition with BBS rims. I loved that car and so did everyone else—it was so slick and clean-looking.

I would take that to the junior lot and park in a safe place where I knew it wasn't in danger, plus, Demi's ex-boyfriend Garrett didn't know what car I had. Garrett and Demi were going out again, but she still liked me, so I had to get mean and call her a rebound whore. That got her off my back, but I told Garrett if he messed with me, I could easily kick his head off. I knew Tyler had my back and with the both of us, we could take out five kids at once. I had bipolar power and he had anger management power, which are the best powers anyone could get. If they took me to the ground, I would easily take control, but standing up, there would be no second chance. The voices in my head were saying to kill him, I didn't want to kill him—just seriously hurt him to where he didn't screw with me again. I never got the chance, because he never challenged me nor did I care, because I would have been expelled or had the cops called on me.

There were a lot of fights at SMA, so cops were always there, either for fights or for kids who failed the drug test. Back in weightlifting, Coach Collis' class, I think he was jealous, because Tyler and I were almost as strong as he was, even though he had been working out for years. We weren't big kids, but we were just strong as oxen.

Tyler and I made a perfect team. Even though we were working out at my house and we were sore, we still had to work out. Tyler forced us to do it, which isn't good on the body, because it doesn't give the muscles enough time to grow. I remember I used to buy these energy drinks called Redline and I would give Tyler one and him only. We were having such an intense workout, until Coach Collis caught us. We were in the locker room and as I was drinking it, he saw me and asked me to hand it over. He said, "This drink is for eighteen and above.

I said, "No, it's not recommended for persons under eighteen, but I can still buy it." He didn't like me arguing with him, so he took me to his office and called my mom and dad. I got the lecture when I got home asking why I think I needed the drink to work out. I let them know that it helps me stay focused. I had a pre-workout drink at my house called White Flood that Tyler and I would share. It has a substance called Beta Alanine that would make our whole body tingle. It was safe and it just felt amazing. We also took Creatine that would put water in our muscles and make them swell up and look more defined.

This was before I started lithium or other medicine. I was obsessed with taking pre-workout formula, vitamins, or Creatine, but never in my life did I take a testosterone booster. I knew that could cut off my natural output, so I never messed around with it nor did I care how it felt. I did try a month's trial of a supplement called Prime. It was supposed to harden the muscles, but after a month of nothing happening, I never took it again.

At the time when I was trying to gain mass, I was taking a protein powder called Up Your Mass. I loved the name and we were going to buffets almost every day after school to try to gain weight. I went on an eating rampage. It was working—I gained more strength, stamina, and drive to work out as hard as I could. Tyler and I had the same amount of strength, which I liked, because it worked out perfectly.

The voices were getting worse and so were the visions, but I tried to ignore them, which sometimes worked. I would hear them saying, "Don't fall asleep during the daytime or we will get you, Stevie boy." They would call me fagot, a loser, and a fat bitch, even though I wasn't even close to being obese—they were just mean voices. Some people have happy hallucinations, but I didn't. Some visions were funny, but that wasn't until later in my life. For now, they were sinister and ominous.

I was going through a deep melancholy. My depression made it so hard for me to get through life, but when I got into the gym with Tyler or my dad, I would push my problems aside and try to have the best workout I could do and make them proud of me, which they were. They must have known I was depressed from the way they acted. I didn't even realize this was the beginning of a big horrendous problem.

I met my good friend, David, at the Military Academy. When I wasn't with Tyler, I was with David, or even if the three of us were hanging out, we all got along just fine. David and I would always play *Call of Duty: Black Ops,* too, except we would play zombies—Tyler like playing live people better. I spent the night at David's all the time and most of the day, while Tyler was working. This was on summer break, because I was still seventeen and in tenth grade. At the time, I was David's chauffeur, because he couldn't drive and didn't have a car. He lived about twenty minutes from me, so sometimes he would stay the night three days in a row. Workouts and *Black Ops* was our lives.

I was always super happy when Tyler could sleep over, too. Tyler and I slept on my bed, while David slept on the bed next to mine. When I would stay the night at David or Tyler's house, every morning when we woke up, we would go to the Waffle House. I was going with Tyler one day and, luckily, he was driving, because in the middle of the road, I saw a bloody woman standing right in front of us. As we got closer, the more I could make out, so I closed my eyes. Once we passed that point, I looked back and she was still standing there. I usually thought hallucinations were blips, but not mine—they were as real as it can get. When Tyler and I got to Waffle House, everyone was speaking a different language. I couldn't understand anyone, so I pointed at the coffee and what I wanted to eat, but thank God, it went away after about fifteen minutes and everything was back to normal.

Summer break at Sarasota Military Academy was my favorite, because I was hanging with a lot of friends and, of course, watching UFC fights on fight night. We would order pizza, but too bad, not beer, since we were all way too young.

Out of all my friends, I loved hanging with Tyler the most—the way we got along and the things we shared in common were just incredible. David and I had a lot in common, but nothing close to Tyler and I. David was in ninth grade when I was in tenth, but I didn't care. We were not too different in age.

David and I took out my golf cart, when a cop passed us. He looked right at us, so I knew he was going to pull us over and sure enough, he did. I pulled off to the side and when he came up to me, he asked for my license. I said I didn't have it, because we were on a golf cart, so he went back and ran my name in the database. He found nothing, but soon, another patrol car pulled up and I'm thinking, *This is great.* David was afraid to death, so I asked the cop if I could show him where I lived. I barely moved, but he asked if I wanted to be arrested twice. I felt like saying how would that be possible, but I kept my mouth shut. Finally, he ordered me to take him to my house, so we went.

When we got there, my mom must have called the president, because there were three cop cars—one down the street, in case I ran and two behind me. My mom asked him what was the problem and he said I could have been arrested. She said she and my father ride in the golf cart all the time, so he threatened to take *her* to jail. My mom went straight to the lieutenant of the police force and asked him if he could get them off our backs— we haven't had a problem since. Now whenever cops drive by, all they do is wave, so we wave back.

I will backtrack to Sarasota Military Academy before the summer when I was in ROTC class with Sergeant Pellegrino about him and my problems. He was a very mean and rude man. He had been in the army and was just an ass. He would throw stuff at people and if he didn't like a paper someone wrote, he would rip it up in front of our faces saying, "You must have shit on this paper—HOOAH!" That was his favorite term. After everything, he said he would say it.

We had a staff sergeant there, who was a student herself, but who thought she was God and that her power gave her gave her the right to order us around. Whenever I would goof off, she would tell me to do pushups. I would say no, then Pellegrino would step in and add fifty more pushups to what I already had, so I would have to do over seventy pushups. I thought I was going to have to complain about him, which I should have done, since he was always cursing at us.

Once, I heard him say to a student, "You must have shit for brains."

I said, "Give her a break, Pellegrino."

He yelled, "What the hell did you just say?" Again I told him to give her a break, but that earned me one hundred pushups non-stop. I just saw it as good exercise, so only to make him madder, I would add in more until finally he said, "Recover." By that time, my arms were very tired.

One day, I was doing my work in class, when I heard a giggle. When I looked up, no one was there except for Pennywise, the clown from Stephen King's book and the movie, *IT*. That white-colored face, red hair, and yellow fangs or teeth scared me so much, I didn't know how to snap out of it. I remember a student next to me asking if I was okay, since I was drenched in sweat. I went to the nurse's office and was sent home for the day.

Along with our uniform, we had to wear the most uncomfortable dress shoes, which would bake our feet in the sun. Pellegrino would make us march two miles, left, left, left, right, left. Our feet were so sore when we got back, some kids took their shoes off. If you did that, then you got pushups. I don't think Tyler or David ever had Pellegrino, which I wish they would have. That would have been a good story for all of us to share with each other. I heard a rumor that Pellegrino threw a chair at a student, but it was probably true. I would not put it past him if he did, because he was such an ass.

I remember I had to get up in front of class and read a report. I was shaking and trembling, but he said, "Suck it up, HOOAH!" I gave him the evil eye and he said, "What are you going to do about it?" I felt like saying, I'm going to kick you in the gonads HOOAH. I would have been expelled, but it would have been worth it.

I didn't plan to stay there anyway. I missed Brickhouse, and I met some good and bad people at SMA, but that's the same at every school. I liked the structure at SMA, but Pellegrino made me want to leave. I did not like that man one bit, but I knew I wouldn't have him for long.

Every time I was having a problem, I would ask to go to the nurse, but he told me to toughen up and that I was too soft. I wanted to complain to the principal, but that would not have worked, since Pellegrino was high up in the army ranks and the principal was, too. They had a lot of respect for each other. I didn't have any friends in that class, nor did I want any, because it was difficult enough to keep up with his class. A friend would have slowed me down and I needed everything I could get to get out of that God forsaken class. I think he had delusions of him being the best sergeant in the world or at least he acted like it. He walked around class like his shit don't stink, to put it in simple terms.

All I've ever known how to write was cursive, but he couldn't read it. I have beautiful cursive, but he would make me get in front of class and read it, probably as some form of punishment, since he knew I had stage fright. I think he had it out for me, because I couldn't do anything to please him. My homework looked like a blind man's writing or I stuttered in front of class. He would call me out on it, saying that stuttering is for bitches and in front of the whole class, he would mock me, but he did some others, too. The class never laughed with him, which made him even more pissed off.

He would stress me out to the point of even more hallucinations that I didn't need. One day, I saw everyone laying with their heads down in a pools of blood and I shook my head and whispered to myself to stop. He heard that and asked me if I was talking to myself, so I said I wasn't. He said, "Bullshit, I saw it with my own eyes!"

I just said politely, "Please, don't worry about me." For some reason, he respected that and left me alone. "Kill him with kindness," my mother would always say. I would not have been surprised if Pellegrino had been bipolar or just dealt with anger management. He had something that turned him an A-hole or maybe he was just a mean guy that didn't want anyone to like him. I didn't care, I just wanted the hell out of his class, but I couldn't for a bit until we switched ROTC instructors.

He hated to be corrected. If he made a grammar mistake or any other kind of error and someone tried to correct him, he would make that person do pushups. If anyone laughed, that was double the amount of pushups. I would always get in trouble for not trying to rank up, but I was there for the education—not going into the army or ranking up, so I stayed a basic until the day I left. Pellegrino always made me fill out paperwork to try to rank up, but I never took it seriously. I would always use the excuse that I lost my paper. Towards the end of his class, I think he started to respect me. I don't know why and I didn't care at all, because all I knew is that the biggest jerk in the school was starting to realize I was a hard worker and wanted to pass his class.

In Pellegrino's class, I was still doing weightlifting and Collis started to respect Tyler and I, too, because he knew we worked out at my house every day and then worked out in his class. He knew it was hard, but we still did it. He pulled me aside one day and I was like, *Oh God, what did I do?* He put his hand on my shoulder and said he was proud of me. I couldn't believe it at the time and I think he pulled Tyler aside, too. We were the strongest kids in the class and some of the best in the whole school. Tyler and I had a lot of kids that would tease us in a good way. I remember before weightlifting, all of us would sit with the rest of the classes before being switched to our stations like P.E., Self Defense, and weightlifting. While we sat there, Tyler and I would start clapping and get all the classes clapping. It was so funny, since Coach Collis would always threaten that the next person would get extra training. Some kids thought it was funny to say, "Happy Birthday, Tyler," and all of them started clapping at once. No one was ever caught, because there must have been thirty kids in there clapping. I started the clapping many times. I loved it and I loved the look on his face when he couldn't find out who was doing it. Finally he said all of us would run laps if we didn't stop. There was no more clapping ever again, because laps sucked. I did think about it though, but I would have gotten beat up.

I had the delusion that I was the best fighter in the world, so I feared no body. I thought if they tried to fight me, they would end up in the gutter. I wasn't a violent kid—I just had violent thoughts and wanted to fight anybody, except a few friends like Tyler, David, Joe, Cohen, Dylan, and Shubby.

Tyler and I were working out one day at my gym, when the lights cut out and I heard a series of loud growls and scratching on the walls. When I snapped out of it, somehow I had ended up outside and Tyler was still working out. I thought good, he didn't see me, so I acted like I was taking a pee. When we were done working out, I went to turn off the radio and Tyler said, "I turned it off, brother."

I said, "It's still playing," but sure enoug, when I got there, it was off. I acted like I was joking with him and he bought it. After Pellegrino, I had another ROTC instructor named Sergeant Browning. I liked him, because he was a good instructor, very nice and well-tempered. I met Dan in that class, and he became my good friend later on after Sarasota Military Academy. We didn't talk much until he went to Brickhouse with me, but I will get to that.

Tyler had two jobs, mowing the grass for his dad's company

and setting up bounce houses for a girl name Jenna. I liked those jobs for him, because he was always happy. Some days were bad, but he held his head up high and pushed through it. Tyler is the strongest kid I know, working in the sun all day like my dad and his dad, Tom. I would have died of heatstroke, if I were ever in the sun like that.

Tyler would work late some days and still make it to school, but I don't think he ever missed a day—I was so happy for him. He was in eleventh grade and I was in tenth, but we are the same age, only he was born a couple months before me. My birthday is July 24 and his is August 14.

I don't have anything much against Sergeant Browning, because his class went by very fast. All I remember is hearing voices and all the rednecks in the school dipping in there, either on the ground, where they would rub it into the carpet or spit in plastic bottles. I thought to myself, I'm never doing pushups in here—ever. When Browning was teaching on the board one day, he had his back to us, when I heard a demonic voice coming from his direction. When he turned around, I thought, *Oh God, he's possessed.* His voice sounded so evil and sinister, it took me a couple seconds to clear it out of my head. I asked to go get a drink and I sort of dragged my butt not wanting to go back to class, but if I didn't go soon, they would suspect something. As usual, after I washed my face and went back to class, everything was fine.

At the time, Dan got kicked out for having failed a test showing he was smoking marijuana. After SMA, he went to Triad, which is an alternative school for truants and people on drugs. I wasn't friends with Dan at the time—I just knew him from class. Tyler and I hadn't sat at lunch together the whole time at SMA, since he would sit with his friends and I would sit with mine. I didn't care, because I got to see him every day anyway, either at my house, his house, or weightlifting. I was out of Soke's class, but occasionally I would skip a class with his permission to go grapple some kids, but you can only do that if you have good grades and a perfect attendance. Soke liked me, so he was always excited to see me grapple. I couldn't slam kids to the ground, which I wanted to do, so I would pick them up to where they let go and then move in for the kill.

Even though I didn't know Dan at the time, I always thought he was a laidback guy, who could become a good friend. I just had a feeling about it. Tyler tried to come over every day, even though he lived so far away, but I would pitch in some gas money every now and then. David would try to come over as much as he could, too, but I was always picking him up, so he would throw in some money to me. He would almost always sleep over. I liked how he worked out every day or every other day.

Tyler was always like my brother since I met him and my favorite person to work out with, and since we lifted the same weight, we would spot each other. Since we were in my gym, we could blast music as loud as we wanted. When Tyler and I would go to the boxing club, we would work our butts off. I was good at the jump rope and also the speed bag, but I also liked to go crazy on the punching bag. Tyler had great technique, since he grew up boxing and I was pretty good, too, from my martial arts background, not as good as Tyler, though I was better at kicks. I remember working out with my friend, Joe. He was in great shape with no fat on him at all. he was a freak of nature. He wasn't as strong and Tyler and I, but it sufficed for the time being.

Tyler and I were working out in my gym one day and black ooze started dripping down the mirror again, but I kept my cool, knowing it would be over soon and it did end eventually. It lasted for about five minutes—one of the *longest* hallucinations of my life. The next day at SMA, I was in Captain Garrett's class and I saw a gun floating in the air, pointing straight at the captain, but I went to the bathroom and cooled off for a little bit. While I was in the locker room getting ready for weightlifting, I saw written in blood on the mirror, "You're Next!" Ironically, a movie came out called, *You're Next*, but all I saw were words written in blood.

My time at the Sarasota Military Academy was everything but enjoyable. I couldn't go through one damn day without hallucinating evil things. I knew I was putting images in my head by watching these horror movies, but that was a risk I was willing to take, because I loved to watch them. Pretty much all my tenth grade experience, I was hallucinating the whole year. I thought it would get better, but it was just the calm before the storm. Tyler told me a story about when a kid stepped on his shoe and meant to do it. Tyler got up and threatened to kick his ass, if he didn't wipe the scuff off his shoe. The kid listened and cleaned his shoe, embarrassing himself in front of his friends.

Before weightlifting, I would always give Tyler a Redline energy drink—the same drink that got us in trouble with Coach Collis, so we would have to sneak them, which we did—it was like a covert operation. For as many times as I was sick, I was really having hallucinations, because I wasn't sick—I just couldn't handle it. I wanted to go home where I felt safe. I wasn't eighteen, just seventeen, so I had to get permission from my family to go home. Some days if I was having problems and I knew they wouldn't send me home, I would sneak out to my car, but usually, there was a watcher to make sure no one snuck out. Then, I would wait patiently for him to drive off, sprint out to my car, and drive off before he came back—he never knew one single thing. That only added to my delusions though.

I thought I was a spy sent on a mission and I really believed that in my head—I felt like a rock star. Sometimes I would pull around to pick up James and go to his house. My grades were excellent, so a few days away from school didn't hurt anything. I knew I could make up the homework if I had to. I always left before math, but only did that like three or four times. It was geometry, instead of algebra. If it had been algebra, I would have left all the time.

I met this girl named Donna in math class, and she was dating an old friend of mine named Toby. While she was dating him, she told me how big of a crush she had on me. I didn't say anything back, because Toby was an old friend of mine. I never told him either, because I didn't want to ruin their relationship. Then I would have made a lot of enemies.

I sort of remember my first big bout of psychosis. I was sitting in math, when I picked my head up, but I saw no one was there, but me—no teacher and no students. I looked around and saw a black demon with red eyes starting to walk close to me, so I ran out of the room. Nothing made sense, because I wasn't at Sarasota Military Academy anymore. I was somewhere completely different, but when I looked behind me, the demon was about twenty feet away. It was speaking in a different language, which sounded like Latin. The next thing I remember, I was in the bathroom looking at myself in the mirror. My friend came in saying, "Captain Garrett wants to see you after class." I was thinking, *Oh Christ, she saw me.* Then after class, she asked if I was all right. She said I was as white as a ghost and she could see me sweating, but luckily, no one else saw me. She sent me to the nurse to check me out and I had a fever of 102. I never told my mom, because I hated going to the doctor, so I just went home and went to bed—that was a very scary experience.

Two things that would always cheer me up were Tyler and grappling in Soke's class. I could channel my anger and frustration to defeat every opponent I faced and destroy them. I never saw Tyler grapple, but I bet he would have been pretty good. He would just have to hold back his anger. I still think bipolar rage is deadlier than anger management, but I would know, because I'm schizoaffective, so I have the worst of both worlds. Later on in life, I was able to channel my rage, but not just yet. I still kind of knew what was going on with me, but I haven't even told my social worker, Scott, at the time, but I think he was the first person I ever told. I felt all right talking about it, because it was only between the two of us, but before I told him, my hallucinations were starting to get worse. I couldn't understand how they could, but they did.

My hallucinations were starting to control my life, because I couldn't go for more than five minutes without having either an auditory or visual one. I thought maybe if I talk to them and give them what they want—attention—maybe they would get bored and leave me alone, so I started to talk to them. I called them my friends, because they were always with me and I was never lonely. They were even my friends when Tyler or David were around, I just didn't speak out loud to them when we would all hang out together, but it didn't matter—they were always with me inside my head. I had names for them, so I would always address each by name, but I forgot what their names were. There was also a demon that would talk to me, which I had a name for, too, but I try to block that out of my head, because it was so evil and hateful, I wanted it out of my head and out of my life.

I loved Sarasota Military Academy, but I had to get out of there. I wasn't safe, even though I knew I was, but I didn't feel it. The only reason I was happy that I went to SMA is because I met Tyler and David, my two friends that were always there for me. My friend, Nolan, and I kind of split apart, because when he got kicked out for marijuana, we never really saw each other after that. I was upset about it, because he was a good friend—just one with a bad habit.

Occasionally when James was still at SMA and Nolan wasn't kicked out, we used to go to Babe Ruth and play ball. Nolan had played some baseball, when he was younger, and even though I was new at it, I could throw a wicked curveball. Once while I was standing at the pitcher mound behind James, I saw Pennywise, the clown again from the movie, *IT*. I sort of stared at it for about thirty seconds, until someone asked, "What the hell are you doing?"

I said, "I thought there was a crow behind you."

He said, "Nope, there's no crow here."

One day I was standing at attention for our morning ritual and I saw a large man standing on the roof yelling at me. I could have sworn it was real, but no one else looked, but he stayed there a good five minutes.

Sometimes if I saw a goofy visual, I would laugh and I was thrown to the back of the line with all of the troublemakers. Pellegrino took me out of line one day, but I thought he was wearing a party hat. I started to laugh in his face and had to do fifty pushups, but it was worth it. I loved that visual—that was pretty much the best visual I've ever had—all the rest were very evil.

I was driving home from school one day and saw a naked bloody lady waving me down, so when I got there, she ran in front of my car and vanished. I was thinking, *Oh hell, tomorrow at school will be a rough one,* but as always, I pushed it aside. The next day I was at school again, ready for my problems. I had an escape route planned, in case I needed to go home early. I knew the exact time when the parking lot monitor left. I remember his name now, Cornel Brockman. I don't think anyone liked him— he was almost like a fat version of Coach Collis, very rude to the students. When he tried to make a joke, no one laughed, which got him even more pissed off, but his jokes were very crude. I forget what they were, but they weren't funny.

Our principal's name was Colonel Dan, so I always wanted to call him Lieutenant Dan from *Forrest Gump,* but I don't think he would find that funny. He was a very mellow laidback guy and I liked and respected him. Sometimes if I got detention, I would go to Colonel Dan and say I couldn't stay, because I had to be somewhere, so he would get me out of it. He probably knew it was a little white lie, but he still let me go. One day I did have to stay though. It was the most boring thing I have ever done. All I would do is read a book, but we weren't even allowed to do that—we had just to sit there and either do homework or wait until the hour and a half was up.

I hated to leave my car parked in the lot all alone, because my friend, Compton, had a redneck truck and we were parked in a bad area. He has had his truck keyed and tires slashed, but I couldn't imagine what he was going through at the time. There was nothing he could do about it, because there weren't any cameras or witnesses. He had it coming to him though, because we were in a bad area and all of his signs and stickers on his car must have offended someone enough to do that to his nice-looking truck. The only funny part is that he still had a razor in his tire, but maybe it was a message saying, "Don't bring that truck back here again or take the stickers off." His truck was custom-made, so I'll bet one tire must have cost four hundred bucks—the wheels were custom, too. I was thanking God that it wasn't my car, even though I didn't have any stickers on mine.

I was always afraid of what if Demi's ex, Garrett, found my car and wanted to get back at me for stealing his girl. I gave her back—no problem, after I found out how crazy and clingy she was. The main reason is that I just wasn't attracted to her anymore. I didn't have that spark I had when I first asked her out. She asked if I thought she was pretty and wanted an honest answer. I told her she was, but I didn't have any feelings for her emotionally and physically. I didn't sleep with her, because I knew it would bite me in the butt in the long run. If I did that, I would never have been able to get her off my back. She was the type of girl that would say she's pregnant just to get me to stay with her and I had no room in my life for that.

Tyler thought she was crazy, too, and I listened to him to get out of that horrific relationship. He might not remember, but I do. He basically saved my life, which we laughed about later. I knew if I ever got into a fight with more than one person, he would back me up, so I love him like a brother. David was my friend, too, but I don't think he would fight too good, because he didn't have any experience in fighting like Tyler and I did.

In Soke's class, when I brought in two pairs of UFC fighting gloves, he would shut the curtain and we would go at it, two at a time fighting—just no headshots and no kicking. Our stomachs were so sore afterwards from the body shots, a couple kids threw up, which was funny, because we weren't giving it our all. I would always fake a left hook then punch straight through their guard with an uppercut to the breadbox. That won the fights for me every time, because no one saw it coming, I was so sneaky with it.

When he opened the curtain, I saw the whole school sitting out in the middle of the gymnasium with gunshot wounds to their heads. There wasn't much blood, but all I remember is talking with Soke to kill time. When I was done and turned around, they were gone. I thought, *How the hell can I help this, if I'm even hallucinating in Soke's class?* After all that fun, why am I still hallucinating. That was the part of the riddle I was never able to solve. It was the enigma in my life that I wanted nothing more but to solve this damn riddle. Was this the work of God, giving me something I couldn't handle? Or did he give it to me, because he knew I could handle it and give me some more insight of the world we live in?

I don't think it's a punishment, but it does suck being Schizoaffective, but in a way, I like it because I'm never alone. I always have my hallucinations with me. Sometimes they talk back to me and I just say to myself, *It'll be over in a little bit*, especially in class if I was having problems, because I can't talk back or acknowledge them or people would find out my secret. I wasn't ready for that at the time, because they would have thrown me into the loony bin, which I always thought would be worse than dealing with it on my own.

Summer after SMA

I WAS SUPER EXCITED WHEN SUMMER CAME, BECAUSE I knew I was finally out of the Sarasota Military Academy. I hung out with Tyler as much as we could hang out—he would sleep over and play *Call of Duty* all night. We would also watch UFC together and go on my golf cart anywhere we wanted. Basically, if he didn't have work, he was always over. He became very strong at working out, as we both were killing it in the gym. Sometimes my dad would join us, which was fun, because he would show us new routines. On the days Tyler wasn't over, David was over and we would play *Call of Duty* all night, too. *Zombies* was David's and my favorite game, because we could play live with other people and we could do that too playing *Team Death Match*. The only thing about *Call of Duty* that Tyler liked was playing live people, but it was very difficult not to die in that game because everyone had their own reaction time.

I played this game called *Fallout 3,* where I would get so into the game that when I turned it off, I would see the characters walking around my house. It was cool at the time, even though I knew it was a serious problem. Shubby and I would hang out too during the summer, but not as much as Tyler, David, and I. During the summer, we would go to the mall almost every day just to watch everyone and what they did—we were pretty much stalkers. We would work out every day or at least, I did, because when and if they weren't with me, I was always with my dad working out.

My biggest fear is my gym attic and still is. My dad would send me in there to gather old photos and one day the light went out. I heard more evil sadistic growls, so I got my butt out of there and told him I was sorry, but I couldn't go in there ever again, so he just handed stuff down for me to grab. I didn't have any problems for the house attic, which made no sense at all, because it was bigger than the gym attic, but I never had any hallucinations in the house attic, although I would never go up there alone.

Every time I had UFC night after the fights, all of us—Joe, David, Tyler, Dylan, Shubby and Cohen—would play manhunt in my yard and I live on three acres with many trees, but outside of the yard was prohibited. We all would stay up until three or four in the morning, but at least we got to sleep in and the next day, get a killer workout in. Even though we were exhausted, we still pushed ourselves to our full potential.

We were so excited that school was over with. I was extremely happy, because after summer break was Brickhouse, my favorite school. I wanted summer break to last forever, because I was having so much fun with all my friends. I had two Joe friends, Joe P and Joe M. I hung out with Joe M the most, because he lived about four miles from me and it was easy to pick him up from his apartment. I felt bad for Tyler, because he was over so much and he lived probably fourteen miles away, so I would throw in gas money and I would try to pick him up or go over there as much as possible. I hated driving unless it was to school and back, because I was afraid of my hallucinations.

I remember driving to David's house once, which I had to because he could not drive. I saw what looked to be a man hitchhiking on the side of the road, but when I came closer, he was throwing up all over the place. I thought I would ask if he was okay, but I would never give him a ride. He was waving to me and then he vanished. I should have known it was a hallucination, but that's how real they all seemed to me. I would also see groups of people standing on the side of the road waving at me, but I didn't wave back. I knew what it was and I wasn't about to let it get me into a car wreck.

When I would stay the night at Tyler or David's house, while I was sleeping on the floor in David's room, I would see creatures crawling after me, so I would put my blanket over my head and try to ignore it. Luckily, we decided to go into the guest room, where I slept on the comfy couch and he slept on the air mattress. I would see the closet door open and I remember the most evil-looking eyes, so I just said to myself, *Okay, Steve, it's okay, it can't hurt you, plus you have your friend in the room with you.*

Whenever I was thirsty or had to use the restroom, I was terrified. One night I went to the restroom and saw written in blood on the mirror, "You can't hide from us much longer until we take you away." I literally thought the devil himself was going to pop through the mirror and take me to hell.

I'm not really a religious person, but after that incident, I went back in the room and prayed for it to stop. I don't know if it was a blip or my prayer being answered, because after that, I was fine and able to go to bed, but I had a nightmare that I was being chased by a big dog. When I woke up, I was drenched with sweat, so I put a towel down and was fine for the rest of the night. I know I put it into my head, because we would always watch horror films. They were bad for my subconscious mind, but I knew it was going to happen anyway, so I thought I might as well enjoy myself while I was with my friends.

I was so excited, because my birthday was coming up—on July 24, I was turning the big eighteen. We had reservations at the Melting Pot, a fondue restaurant. I invited Tyler, David, and Shubby, plus my amazing parents came. Before we went, I stayed the night at Tyler's house, where we watched *Daybreakers* and *Jeepers Creepers*. I had enough hallucinations to bother the hell out of me, so I was thinking, can't I just have a break, since my birthday is tomorrow, but nope, I had to have problems. As I said before, the only movie that scares me is the movie, *The Fourth Kind*.

The night before my birthday at Tyler's house, we watched his favorite movie, *Signs*. I loved that movie, too, but it didn't scare me like *The Fourth Kind*. If I thought now was bad, I had no clue what was in store for me after my eighteenth birthday. The next day, Tyler and I went back to my house, since he had picked me up on the way. We picked up David, since he lives near Tyler and went to my house, where Shubby drove over and my mom, of course, took all our pictures.

We played *Call of Duty*, switching turns and finally it was time to go to dinner. Shubby was out of it the whole time, because he had never been to such a fancy dinner before. It's almost as if he wasn't there with us. It was pretty hilarious, but he ate like a lion that had just captured a gazelle. But we couldn't leave dinner without the chocolate fondue dessert.

Everyone stayed the night, so we all watched Chucky movies and poor Shubby was again up all night. As I said, he's very superstitious and believes there are zombies back where he grew up. After we were good and scared, we played *Call of Duty*.

We didn't have much summer left, but after my birthday, my mom surprised me with an amazing gift. She said she was going to buy me a tattoo, which I had always wanted. We went to a shop called Level Five. I wanted a black and red superman symbol tattoo right across my spine on my upper back, but I was worried about the pain. It did hurt, but not nearly as bad as I thought it would. I was sitting right underneath a vent, so I was shivering. The tattoo artist thought I was in pain and let me go to the bathroom and take a break before we start up again, so I agreed, but when I got back, the adrenaline was gone, so that was the only part that hurt. Everyone loved my tattoo. Tyler liked it the most, because he had always wanted a tattoo, but didn't know what he wanted, plus, he was afraid of the pain, so I told him it feels like a cat with sharp nails scratching across your skin.

My tattoo took an hour and a half of sitting there that long with a needle penetrating my skin. It did hurt a bit, but in the end, it was all worth it, knowing it was there for the rest of my life. David was with me while I was getting my tattoo, but I don't know where Tyler was at the time, but I wished he were there watching it.

I asked to take another break to use the bathroom, so I went in to wash my face and go pee, but when I got out, everyone was invisible. I could see the tattoo gun floating, ready to tattoo again, so I went over to the chair, sat down, and the tattooing started up again. I could hear him talking to me, but I couldn't see him, so I just acted like everything was okay and finally, after about five minutes, I was back to normal where I could see everyone again. That was one of the longest hallucinations I have ever been through, but it was only the beginning. The tattoo artist said my back barely bled, which was good, because he didn't have to keep wiping blood off as he was tattooing. Before the tattooing was over, on the mirror I saw a reflection of myself and where David was. I slowly looked over and he was sitting, quietly watching what was going on. I was thinking, *I need to get the hell out of here,* but it was almost done.

My mom peeked in to see how it was going, which was nice, because I felt safe around her. I also felt safe with David there, but not as much as with my mom. I wished my dad could have come, but he was working, while my mom was on lunch break. I laughed, because when the artist first started my tattoo, David was standing over me. The artist goes, "Back the shit up, man, you're blocking my view." I tried not to laugh and mess it up, but it was too hilarious. I could tell David was embarrassed, but he hid it well.

Before he was finished, I had one final visual of bloody footprints walking towards me and stopped when it got to me. I heard a growl so evil and sinister that when we finished and he put a bandage on me, I paid him quickly and got the hell out of there. When I got home, I took the bandage off and stared at my tattoo. It was so bright and beautiful, I couldn't help but stare. Mom put lotion on it, so it healed better, with no bad side effects, like fading or premature peeling. I was scared when it started to peel in the shower. It was black and red and I thought, *Oh God, this isn't good,* but the artist had warned me that it was natural, so that made me feel better.

As summer was starting to end, I went through some melancholy, because it was such a good summer, but I know back at Brickhouse is where most of my friends were and Tyler would take classes at Brickhouse, too, so I just tried to enjoy the rest of the summer as much as I could.

David was going to Riverview High School and Tyler was finishing twelfth grade at the Military Academy. Even though we were going to be split up, we all remained best friends. The rest of the summer, Tyler and I spent a lot of time together. Sarasota Military Academy gave out a lot of homework, so I knew he would be occupied with school and either would have to do homework here or at school to get it over with. Then he could come over for a couple hours

Before all that started, we wanted to play all the *Call of Duty* we could and work out as much as we could together. He was such a strong kid, he almost out did me. My dad and he were enough inspiration for me, since they were both strong as hell. I was falling behind a bit, but I caught up. Somehow I had a watchful eye over me that helped me get through tenth grade and all the problems I was having and my GPA didn't suffer at all. Though there were a lot of problems at SMA, I never got caught up in any trouble unless I had to.

I didn't mention the fights at SMA, but there was a fight every week. Some included my friends, but I still couldn't get involved. I didn't want to get a ride in the back of a police car from butting in, when it wasn't my business. I had a couple of weeks to go before I went back to Brickhouse, but I was so sick. It was probably from stress knowing I was about to start a new grade. I thought there was going to be all new faces and so my hallucinations were even more horrible—I would say the worst I've had, but that would be a lie.

When I went to my window, I saw a Mexican gang starting to walk up my driveway. At that point if I had access to my 9mm, I would have gone out to kill me some gang members, but of course when I went out, there was nobody there. When I came back in, I heard a series of gunshots, so I went right back out, thinking I was going to die, but again nobody was there. That was how sick I was.

The week before Brickhouse began, I was starting to lighten up a bit, because I knew I would feel a lot safer going to a small school like that. Also, I had a car and I was eighteen, so I didn't have to ask permission to leave school. All I had to say was, "I'm sick and I need to go home," and they would evaluate me and then send me home. I wasn't going to do it all the time—just on bad days, which I knew were going to happen, and maybe even worse.

Back to Brickhouse

FINALLY, THE FIRST DAY OF MY ELEVENTH GRADE AR-rived. I was super excited to see most of my friends from ninth grade, including Shubby, Andrew, Erin, Robert, Cameron, and Josie. All of them were in the twelfth grade, so I knew next year, they would be graduated and away from Brickhouse.

Mrs. Brickhouse, the owner, had died of old age. Mrs. Detra, who was the middle school teacher, became the new principal and she was an amazing one. She was nice and funny and always had a smile on her face. Mrs. Wilkes, the science teacher, had moved away and our new teacher was Mrs. Whitley. What a beautiful woman! We all took turns hitting on her, but she never cared— she would just laugh along. Shubby hit on her the most, saying some crude things and he was the only one sent to Mrs. Detra for his remarks. I wasn't too far behind from being sent out, too. The next day, Shubby was back at it with his remarks, so back to Mrs. Detra he went. This time, he got a detention two to six, which was horrible. I know, because I got it once and I was bored out of my mind. The only difference is we could bring a book in to read, while SMA didn't allow anything but looking at the wall.

Mrs. Cordovez was still there, only this time, she had her eyes on Shubby to make sure he didn't mark up her back with Sharpie markers. Instead of the desks being in a circle where she was an easy target, she moved the desks to be in lines of three and there were probably six to a class. Shubby found a new tactic to get at her. He brought in a high-power laser pointer and when she turned around, he would point it at her butt, making the whole class laugh. He was pointing it at her head once and instead of the laser being green, it was red. I saw a bullet going in slow motion right to her head, so I went straight to the bathroom, telling myself it wasn't real, but when I went back to class, she was lying dead on the ground. I went back to the bathroom, washed my face, and when I got back, she told me never to go again without permission.

I never laughed at the laser pointer after that episode. Mrs. Christina was still there—she was the overweight Polish lady who never looked at me once, since the Coke accident, because she hated me so much. I heard her grunt every time she walked past me, and when I finally looked at her and made a fart noise, she went straight to Mrs. Detra's office. She said I needed a detention, but Mrs. Detra liked me, so I never got a detention—she just told me to ignore Mrs. Christina.

The most hated teacher in the school was Miss Esperonza, and of course I had reading with her and Shubby was there with me—just him and me. We couldn't mess with her, because she was right next to us. We read a whole book about Mount Everest, taking turns. I had many hallucinations in that class, as it was almost unbearable. One of the most memorable ones is when I picked my head up off the desk, yawning, and I looked over, but saw no one there. I got up and walked out of the cubical, but no one was around, so I panicked. I went back to the cubicle and closed my eyes and wished it to be gone soon.

This lasted about five minutes and when I came out of it, I was leaning into my hands and Miss Esperonza was looking straight at me and so was Shubby, but nothing was said between us. I must have been acting weird the whole time, because they looked kind of shocked, but I didn't want to know what I did or what I looked like. I must have gotten out of my seat without permission. If I did, why didn't they stop me or break me out of my trance? Was I really that bad off and they were afraid to snap me out of it? I'll never know, because they never said anything, but those terrified looks on their faces said it all.

Finally she asked, "Why don't you get something eat?" I was starving, so I got two pop tarts and a Coke. Luckily I didn't spit Coke in her face or I would never hear the end of it nor would she want me as a student anymore.

Every time she went to the bathroom, Shubby and I would always joke around. This is crude to say, but one day, he spit in her chair and rubbed it around so it didn't look like spit. When she sat down, we lost it and she didn't know what we were laughing at, but she wasn't pleased. She never found out a damn thing, which was good for us, because I don't know what would have happened. I'm sure that would have landed us in four-hour detention or worse, a suspension. My parents would have killed me if they found out what we did.

Shubby and I had every class together, which didn't bother me, but it was a distraction. That meant I would have to pay close attention to everything that was being taught, so I could get a good grade, since I always excelled in every grade, except math.

Miss Esperonza and Shubby would get into fights, but they were always verbal, thank God, but it wasn't pretty. He would curse and rage and have to go home for the day. I love Shubby, but he was always a distraction. I was able to get so much more work done with him gone and the teachers were at ease when he was not there. I thought this was hilarious, but not all the time.

We were in Miss Esperonza's class, when he got into another fight with her, calling her a bitch, and that set her off. Finally, I just said, "Shubby, go home and relax," which he did. He stormed out of the cubicle and drove home with no permission. Then they were mad at me for telling him to go home, because I had no right to do that. That's when I just asked, "I got him out of your hair, didn't I?" They looked at each other, relieved, and ended up saying, "Thanks, Steve."

The next day, Shubby would face the jury with another four-hour detention. Andrew and I didn't have Miss Esperonza together any more, but we had English together with Miss Geanette. I despised that woman, but Andrew would call her out on all her flaws. She hated him, even though she never said a word, but I could tell from her body language. I don't think anyone liked her, because she was such a jackass. She would try to make jokes, but they weren't funny and she made weird noises like cat purring and hissing. No matter what she did, she just wasn't funny.

I remember one day she walked out of the room and Shubby always thought it would be funny to turn off the lights and yell, so Mrs. Whitely would have to jump into the room to see what was wrong. One day when he turned the lights off, I felt a huge crack on my forehead and saw little fairies floating around my head. When the lights were turned back on, Shubby had thrown a trashbin across the room, which had hit my forehead. That was the closest I had ever been to being knocked out. I wasn't mad at him though, because he didn't mean to hit me, so we just laughed. A little trickle of blood was running down my forehead. She knew who it was right away, but we never ever snitched on one another.

Shubby got a four-hour detention, which he was always complaining about, but I told him he had brought it upon himself by acting like that. I was very lucky he didn't hit my nose or he would have broken it for sure. I did have a migraine the rest of the day, so I went home early and went to bed with a horrible pain in the left side of my prefrontal lobe. It was great being eighteen, because I could go up to the desk and say I needed to go home and they didn't have ask any questions about why, so I just went straight home.

I was sitting in Miss Geanette's class one day, when I saw a figure walk by the classroom, so I acted like I had to go to the restroom. When I walked out, it was a man with the back of his head missing like he had been shot. Since it was a small school,

I followed him, but I didn't have far to go. Finally I made it to Mr. Dillon's class, where the man went out the back door. He was waving me on, but I didn't follow. I just told myself that it was a hallucination, so don't worry about it.

When I got back to Miss Geanette's room and sat down, the man was standing behind the door gawking at me. I felt uncomfortable, so I went to the front desk and asked for some Benadryl, thinking maybe it would calm me for the time being, but it only sedated me. I felt like I was in a horror film, but could not shake the feeling of being watched, nor could I control it—I just had to tough it out until it finally dissipated.

The next day in her class, I saw a disfigured body hanging from the ceiling and I wanted to say, "Don't you people see this?" But I couldn't do that, because that would have earned a phone call to my mom and possibly a trip to the psycho ward, which was not an option for me at all. I had so many problems in her class, but I will get back to that.

After Miss Geanette, I would have reading with Miss Esperonza, while Mrs. Whitely was English, but I liked both classes. I felt safe in Miss Esperonza's class, because it was just Shubby and I and a cubicle surrounding us, so I didn't have to worry about something coming up and attacking me from behind. I felt bad for her, because of how much Shubby would make fun of her when she was gone. Once he tried to put a tack on her chair, but I told him that was idiotic, because it was just us in the class. She liked me, so she would know it was you, but it would have been pretty damn funny.

I tried to live in the moment, because next year, they would all be gone and in college or at least some of them. My friend, Cameron, wanted to go to culinary school, which I still hope he is doing okay down there in Johnson & Wales. He would always bring in fresh-made fudge, which was amazing how he made them in such a short period of time, because they were delicious.

Both of Mrs. Brickhouse's grandsons, Robert and Henry,

were there—they were good kids. Robert was a friend of mine, not a good friend, but he was there to talk to, if I wasn't doing too good. Even though I was at small school, I always felt like I was being watched, because my paranoia was getting worse. At one point, I thought I had a warrant out for my arrest. I was so afraid to leave the house, especially to go to school. I thought for sure I was going to be arrested and locked up for a while. I would sometimes have Tyler drive us around, which made me feel so much better. I had nobody to drive me to school, except for Shubby coming to pick me up. When we got back to my house, Shubby and I would play *Call of Duty*, until he had to leave.

At this point, I was having hallucinations many time a day. No matter what I did, they would follow me, especially if I was alone—I didn't feel safe anywhere at any time. They were just so evil: demons, skeletons, dwarfs, goblins, midgets, shadow figures, and much more. I was living in a nightmare, so I knew sooner or later, I would have to tell my parents, but just wasn't ready yet. I thought I would never be ready in my life to expose my secret.

I wasn't worried about my parents thinking I was on drugs, because they could easily drug test me and know I wasn't. However, I wished I was on hallucinogenics, because then I would know I would be fine within a couple hours. Some say I'm lucky to be able to hallucinate or be manic, but in reality, it sucks. If I could keep mania for the rest of my life without sinking into deep depression, I would. I get all of this for free—the mania, the hallucinations—it's all-free and some people pay good money to hallucinate and feel great euphoria. I've never tried meth before, but from what I have heard, it makes you feel great. Mania and euphoria—I get it for free, so all I need to do is quit my meds and in over a week, I would be high as a kite soaring through the air.

I like to think of it as a pinball machine. The lever shoots the ball into mania land and as it bounces around, those are mixed episodes of paranoia and hallucinations. You're trying to keep the ball from going through the flippers, because when the ball does make it through, that's what deep depression is. When I go through my depression, I wish I would be taken away from this world, because I feel like I don't fit in at all.

I don't have emotions, so guilt is the best way to put it. I don't want to tell my parents, because then they would worry about me too much and I don't want that to happen. I didn't tell my friends, because I was worried I wouldn't have friends, if they thought I was crazy. However, that wasn't the case, which I later came to realize.

I was still friends with a lot of kids from Sarasota Military Academy and I stayed close to them my whole eleventh grade year. I would still host UFC fight night, if they paid their share of it. Dylan, whom I met at Brickhouse, would always come over to watch it. He was big into mixed martial arts and knew a lot of good moves. When I first met him, we sort of didn't like each other. He was two grades ahead of me, but when I was in the eleventh grade, we became good friends. He had already graduated, but I didn't care, because he was a cool, fun guy to hang out with.

One of the biggest surprises is when I found out that Tyler was taking a few classes at Brickhouse, too. He was taking English with Miss Geanette, Spanish with Miss Cordovez, and history with Mr. Dillon. I had quite a few classes with my brother to joke around with, even though we both needed to concentrate and would get the evil eye from all the teachers.

He disliked Miss Geanette, too, along with everyone else. I was passing by Miss Geanette's class one day and had a visual of her on a stripper pole swinging around. I went to the bathroom, puked a couple times, and walked past again, but she was sitting in her chair grading papers. Where that delusion came from, I had no idea, but it scarred me for life. I still can't get it out of my head. Luckily she was fully clothed, but I can't imagine what I would do, if she weren't.

One day there was a hint of someone bringing drugs into the school, so we all had to go up front, while the K9 sniffed our backpacks. I don't think they found anything, except for some cigarettes that were hanging on the outside of someone's back-pack. Someone lucked out that day or they would have had a trip in the back seat of the police car.

I was paranoid that someone or something would put some-thing in my bag, so I always kept it right next to me in plain sight. I was friends with almost the whole high school there, so I knew no one would ever do that to me, but I was still paranoid that they might "spike the punch," meaning plant something in my bag like marijuana or worse, pills, which would be a felony. I heard someone say they hid the drugs in the ceiling, the type you could push up using your pinky.

I never did anything—not that I was afraid to, but it would be snitching and I would never snitch, if it would do harm to another person. We found beer sitting up in the ceiling, prob-ably from the construction workers, but it was starting to leak through the ceiling. Luckily, it didn't do damage to the ceiling, but sadly, the beer could not be saved—it was a tragic loss. We never found out whose beer it was, but we had a pretty good idea that it was the construction workers, because who else would put beer in the ceiling?

When I came back into Miss Geanette's room, I saw blood dripping from the ceiling and walls. It was like the movie, *The Shining*, by Stephen King. Blood was everywhere pouring from the walls. I would also see bugs crawling around me, so I just closed my eyes and asked for it to go away. Then I felt them crawling up my leg, so I just asked God to take it away. Three minutes later, it was gone. I still had the creeps after it went away.

After that was Miss Esperonza's class. I liked her class because it was just Shubby and I and I knew it was safe. However, I still had hallucinations, like seeing black ooze coming out of her eyes and large teeth every time she smiled at me. Maybe she wasn't smiling at all, but I still saw large evil bloody teeth.

We would read our book taking turns, but I hated trying to read, because the words on the page would start to float off the paper and circle around her head, so I couldn't read. I would say, "Let Shubby read some more—I have a bad headache." Sometimes I would ask to go home and get the hell out of there just to get these hallucinations to stop. The next day in her class was the same damn thing—more hallucinations. I started to wonder if they would ever go away on their own.

I remember walking by Miss Geanette's room and seeing her hanging with a noose around her neck, but I just said, "Stop!" knowing it was a visual. I walked on, but when I came back by again, she was still there hanging, I didn't know what to do, so I went to the front desk and asked for a strawberry pop tart. After I ate it and walked by again, there she was reading a school paper. I felt very relieved, as I always was when they went away.

I always had good grades in all my classes, which I never understood, because I was having so many problems. My smarts took me far, even though everywhere I went, I was having problems. Miss Esperonza deserved what Shubby did to her, because she was a mean lady—not really to me, but she was still rude. She would never let anyone go to the restroom or to get Advil, if we had a headache. I should have never stopped him from putting the tack under her, but like I said, she would have known it was Shubby, because she would know I would never do something like that, and Shubby would have probably been suspended. I would have been in trouble, too, for not saying anything about it and letting her get hurt, because she would have to have had a tetanus shot, because it wasn't a clean tack—he got it from the board, so it would have been an infection waiting to happen. There could have been a lawsuit against him, if she had been hurt badly. She probably wouldn't do that to him, but then again, I wouldn't put it past her if she did.

Finally after many days of going home, Mrs. Detra asked if I was okay and why I was leaving so much. I just told her I had bad anxiety and some days it was so bad, I couldn't focus on schoolwork, but she bought it without me telling her I was hallucinating every day I was there.

I was talking to her one day and while I was looking right at her, her eyes turned black as the night. I was staring right into her soul, because if I looked away or walked away, she would be right up my ass in a matter of seconds. Then I would have to do the whole act of saying, "Sorry, Mrs. Detra, I forgot something in the classroom," or tell her I had to get something or go to the bathroom—I didn't feel like playing that game. I know if I told her, I would get a couple of days away from school, but then, I would have so much homework to make up, it wouldn't be worth it.

I already had to make up so much work from just missing a day, I couldn't imagine what a week would look like, especially in Mr. Dillon's class. He never taught—he would just give us class work to do. He wasn't a good teacher at all, but he thought he was. Many students complained about him, but Mrs. Detra wouldn't do a thing about it. He always looked forward to the end of class, so he could have a smoke and let loose all his troubles that we were causing him, even thought he had the easiest job—just giving class work to do without teaching the class.

I put my head down one day and went into another bout of psychosis. When I picked up my head, I saw nobody there with me. Mr. Dillon was gone, along with the whole class. I freaked out and ran to the couch in front of the school and still saw nobody. Everyone was gone, so I just sat there hoping it would all be okay. I sat on the couch and counted to one hundred and opened my eyes to Mrs. Detra standing over me, asking if I was all right or if I needed to go home. I told her that I needed to go home, but instead, I went to the park near my house and swung on the swings, trying to get back to land of the living.

It was one of the parks where James and I went to play baseball, so I had many fond memories of being there and it made me happy. It was also the park I brought my girlfriend to at the time. James and I would swing and see who could do the most pullups on the monkey bars and play Home Run Derby before they blocked it off for the Orioles to do their spring training, so we were forced to go to Babe Ruth to play baseball. I liked to play catch the most though, because it's good for hand and eye coordination and I liked to practice my curve ball and fast pitch.

Sometimes when I was playing, I would visualize birds flying in front of me or people watching me play baseball. I knew it was a hallucination, because when I told James, he said nobody was there and asked if I was okay, so I acted like I was joking, but I don't think he bought it. If I really had to tell him about my problem, I would, but I didn't trust him fully yet.

I always thought if I didn't tell anyone, maybe it would go away. However, that only made matters worse, because I was keeping it locked up inside my head. I know you're supposed to tell people things like that, but I still couldn't trust anyone else, but my parents. I still haven't told them at this time, because I felt they would throw me in jail or a mental institution.

James had dropped out of school at the time, because he and was working on his GED at the time, so he was always free during and after school, if I ever had to go home. We would play catch, which was therapeutic for me, if I was having problems. It was hard to go home at times, because my grandpa lived with us, so I just said I had a free day or school let out early. I knew he wouldn't be able to tell the difference, so I would come home and play video games or go see James.

On the really bad days, I would go home and sleep, trying to knock out my hallucinations. If I slept in the middle of having an auditory or visual, I would have horrible nightmares of my parents leaving me alone with problems forever. I would wake up seeing them and was so relieved, but I hated to go back to sleep. I knew I would have more nightmares, since I was still hallucinating before I went to sleep.

Some nights I would stare at the wall having visuals and seeing creepy crawlers and snakes on the ground. I was mesmerized at what I was seeing—I don't know why, but I was fascinated and starting to wonder if I was even alive anymore—is this life after death? I couldn't sleep, because I was afraid and I couldn't stay awake, because I was afraid I was stuck in hell or purgatory, waiting to find out my fate.

I kept having a delusion that God put me on earth to do something, what it was, I didn't know, but I felt I had these problems for a reason. Maybe God put me here to see how much crap I could handle and to see if I was worthy enough to go to heaven, but I knew that wasn't true, because why would God do this to me to test me? I didn't believe it, but I had to believe in something. I was never mad at God but I was frustrated on why do I and other people have these problems, so I'm not alone, but for a long time I thought I was alone.

Mrs. Detra let me go home. Because it was on a Friday, I had the whole weekend to let off steam and confront my visuals. I told myself, *It's time to confront my fears,* but that's hard to do when you're terrified of what's going to happen next. My hallucinations had been bad all weekend, so I was afraid to go to school Monday, but I said my prayers and went back anyway.

After the receptionist, Karen, left, we hired a new one named Marcy. I liked her a lot, because when I asked to go home, she never asked why, even though I would never have told her in the first place. I didn't care if I got into trouble going to the park, because it always got my mind off things by just swinging and sitting on the slide, thinking about life and why I had this illness.

I didn't have a diagnosis at the time, but I knew something was terribly wrong. Not only was my schizophrenia getting worse, but so was my bipolarity, and the rage was starting to kick in. I remember when Shubby ordered pizza once and I thought it would be funny to poke holes in his pizza. When he found out, he freaked and started yelling at me, but I jumped over the table and let loose my rage on him. I could see the fear building up inside of him—I would have been afraid of me, too, since I was two times bigger than he was. After I calmed down, we hugged and that was it—there was no more fighting, because he was my best friend and I would never do that to my best friend—I just lost my temper.

After Mrs. Detra heard all the commotion, she ran in and made sure we were okay. We just said we were playing around and she goes, "Save it for out of school." Even some of the school kids came in, probably hoping for a fight, but I would never fight my best friend. At the time, I was going through a bout of paranoia thinking people were looking at me or reading my thoughts, so I tried not to think the whole time I was there, but I couldn't help but think, so I was in hell.

Tyler and I would go to the mall every weekend to try to scope out girls, but I was too sick at the time to worry about girls. Every Friday or Saturday, we would go to CiCi's pizza for the All You Can Eat special. We would make a pile of crust to see who could eat the most and he always won. My favorite was the cinnamon frosting dessert. Still, I couldn't help but feel alone in the world, even though I had my wonderful parents and great friends. I was living a lie and never telling anyone, but I thought it was for the best at the time.

I didn't like my picture ever being taken, because I thought the flash would give me a seizure, even though I've never had one before. I also thought the flash of the camera would sneak into my soul. It was a weird delusion I know, but at the time, it was real to me.

Eleventh grade was not as bad as tenth grade, but I was just going through the eye of the storm. I mean it was calm and I hoped it would last, but it didn't.

This girl named Josie, who I saw at Sarasota Military Academy, was also in Brickhouse, but she was a senior. I built up the courage to ask her on a date, so we ate and went to see a movie—it was one of the best dates I've ever had. She was such a beautiful girl, brunette hair and amazing body, but we only went on one date before we realized we were not compatible with each other. I was a bit bummed, but stress also triggers my hallucinations.

At that time, I also met my friends, Austin and Norman, who were real party goers. I never wanted to go to a party, because it made me nervous—all those people drinking and partying—it's just too much for me. They were good friends though, and we were always joking around in class until the teachers told us to shut up. Since it was a small school, we pretty much had every class together, which was fun.

Earlier I brought up Shubby almost putting a tac on Miss Esperonza's chair. Well, he finally threw one on the ground and she stepped right onto it. When she let out a scream, Mrs. Detra came running out to see what was going on. God, it was funny, but she was in a lot of pain. Shubby and I couldn't help but laugh our butts off under our breath. My laughing didn't last too long, because soon after that I heard a demonic cackle right behind me. I slowly turned around and saw blood on the wall saying, "Condemned." I never laughed in her class again, even if it was funny as hell. It was just too evil for me to let go of easily.

That wasn't the last time I saw or heard the word, condemned. I would also see and hear footsteps on the walls or I would hear footsteps coming above the ceiling. I could easily ignore those, but the evil ones I couldn't—they were too terrifying. I always thought I would be good at writing a horror novel or film from all I saw in my head. I knew I would be good at it, but I just never really sat down to write out the characters, nor would I know where to start.

In eleventh grade, I was having some hallucinations, but it was mainly the depression. I hate being depressed—I'd honestly rather have hallucinations than that, but I didn't have to wish for hallucinations to come, because they were right behind, just waiting to pop through at any moment. Then came the mania that lasted about two weeks this time. I was able to write my homework during class, while listening to the teacher for another task. There wasn't anything I couldn't do at the time—I was flying high as a kite and didn't want it ever to leave my system. I was in full throttle and it's as if I have a full-on fight or flight response. Nothing could hurt me, I didn't feel pain too much, and I had tunnel vision at the time, but I knew it was going to be short-lived. I would get straight A's on my homework assignments and on class work, but I was still having visuals. The mania was full-blown, so I didn't care about a thing, but the demonic voices and visuals would soon bring me back to reality.

I hated to go to the bathroom, because I would see evil figures in back of me in the mirror. One day I was walking to the bathroom and saw Chucky run in there and close the door, so I went back to class. When I heard the door open, I told Miss Geanette I had to go then, since they went out, but, of course, when I got there, I saw Chucky sitting on the floor, so I just said, "Screw it!" and went in anyway, because I had to go to the bathroom, so too bad to give a damn. When I got back to class, I saw Chucky sitting in my chair, so I went to the couch and sat complaining of headache. Miss Marcy gave me a Coke on the house, which was very nice of her. I chugged that down and went to class, but Chucky was gone. I had my seat back, but I wasn't far behind, because I had been able to listen to Miss Geanette from the couch, because she talks so loud. I was in such full-blown mania, I thought I could do anything and not have to deal with any consequences.

When Miss Cordovez took us back over to the Spanish bakery, I snuck a monster. When she caught me, I said, "Too late, I already drank it." Little did she know I was worse off without it, because sometimes caffeine calms me down. They had the best-baked goods there, because everything was fresh-made and hand-made. I also tried this Mexican soda. It was so good, I bought another one for when we went back to class. I poured Shubby a small cup of it, because he would do the same for me, if it came down to it, plus Coke was a dollar, so I could have one anytime I wanted. Luckily, my mania caused me never to have a sugar crash while I drank all this Coke.

In Miss Geanette's class, whenever it was time for me to read, I would be reminded to slow down, because I was reading too fast, but I was flying high again. This was about day five of my manic episode. I couldn't stay still and it actually caused me to go home one day, because if I was manic and didn't move, the rage came and I wasn't fun to be around then. I went home, worked out, and played my video game, and even tried to take a nap, but that was out of the question. Finally, three o'clock rolled around, which is when my dad gets home from work, so I had another workout with him. Now I had two intense workouts and was still ready to go on a full journey.

I could do anything I wanted to do when I was manic. My grades increased and I was a monster, when it came down to schoolwork. When we had spelling and grammar tests in Miss Geanette's class, it only took me probably three hours of studying before I knew them, but I just wanted to make sure they were engraved in my head. I never scored below a ninety while I was manic. Even when I wasn't manic, it just came naturally to me, but I took a lot more studying that I didn't need to do, if I was manic. Everything was so much easier and straightforward when I was manic. When I went home, I would wait for my dad to get home to work out. The mania gave me incredible workouts that I felt like I was on meth. I had such energy and drive, I thought I would never be able to stop working out.

It's hard to explain what mania is, but it's like sticking yourself with pure adrenaline times one-hundred. Everything is possible when you're manic and it feels like you can run a marathon over and over again until you die, but you wouldn't be able to tell, because you're in such a zone. The sense of pain goes away and you get tunnel vision. Your hearing increases and it's almost like you develop superhuman strength and heightened senses—it's just incredible. It was lasting so long, I was barely sleeping maybe two hours a night.

I knew it wouldn't end well, but I was trying my best to keep it. I only had about twenty-four hours of sleep within two weeks, but that's before my mania left. I could read a four-hundred page book in two days, if I really tried to concentrate. I was a prisoner, stuck behind the mania bars. No matter how much I loved it, even before I knew about this disease, I knew that it would all come to an end. I knew from reading my medical books that I had to be bipolar, but where were these hallucinations coming from? That was an enigma that I couldn't solve, but I still didn't ask for help.

I used to like driving around Sarasota in my truck. My dad gave me his 2005 GMC Z71. I loved that truck so much, I would drive it everywhere. It was sort of therapeutic and I still do it to this day, although I have a different car now, but that didn't happen until later. At school, I would have to park my truck far away at the end of the lot, because I was not good at parking it at all. Pretty much all the rednecks there drove huge trucks and I was amazed on how well they handled them. My friend, Compton, the kid who got his tires slashed, went to Brickhouse, too. He had a jacked-up black truck. I never knew the brand, because it was blacked out.

His family owned a night club called Joyland, very popular, so many people go there every night, except me, because I wasn't of age yet. He invited me when I turned eighteen, but I still didn't go. I'm not much of a partier, plus, I couldn't drink at the time, so what's the fun in that. I don't like to dance and I do not like places that blare loud music—just never been a fan of that, because loud music ups my anxiety and also kind of brings up my mania. I get very mad, and I've even been to a couple of concerts and it just makes me nervous. Too loud of music makes me hallucinate, but confuses me to where I want to leave right away even if we just got there.

I'm more of a laidback type of guy. I like to hang out and watch movies and sometimes go out, but I hate it, especially if I don't know the person and if there is a large crowd of unknown people. There are just a lot of shady people at parties and I don't feel comfortable going out.

Yes, I know I'm boring, but I can't help it. I wish I was more social, but I don't like it when I'm forced to go into a situation that I'm not comfortable with. I always need an exit strategy to know I will be safe in any situation, if it ever came to that.

I've heard too many stories of cops crashing parties and I don't want to be arrested for just being there at the wrong time. It doesn't matter who you are or if you were drinking or not, you would still be arrested for suspicion of underage drinking. If it ever came to it, I would be the designated driver. I've only been to one party— so crowded, loud music, and people yelling, so I made us leave right away before there was any drinking. Luckily. we were not in my truck, because if the cops were to come, they would identify it. Then, if they saw me in it on the streets, I'd be pulled over and they would know that me and my truck were there.

Tyler never forced me to go anywhere I didn't want to go. I respected him so much for saying that there were certain times I wanted to socialize, but a party is not that place, with a bunch of drunk people puking and having alcohol poisoning—it was a bad scene. I didn't drink, but you don't have to drink to have fun, but I felt so left out. Everyone in high school thinks you need to drink to have fun and let loose, but not me, and I also knew it would hurt my parents if I ever did. I didn't have to drink or do drugs to have good time. All I had to do is wait for my mania to pop back in and I was set and alive and an adrenaline junky.

I used to go on Tyler's dirt bike with him all the time. We would cruise down his street, because no one was up that late. I'm sure when we rolled by, it woke them up for it was a very loud bike that I wasn't used to. That loudness coming from the bike infuriated me, but I stayed calm and just tried to enjoy the ride.

Whenever I would stay the night at Tyler's, we would have a huge bonfire in his backyard and drive around the bonfire doing burnouts on his truck. we would drift around the intersection of his street, because we knew no one was there. After the bonfire, we would go for a ride to an unknown destination, just ride all night with the windows rolled down.

Sometimes we would go to 7-11 to get Monsters and try to stay up as long as we could. That was bad, because staying up later after I hit a certain point is when my mania kicks in and I don't get any sleep—not even an hour. I didn't care though, because the next day I was manic in all ways. This was on a Friday night, so luckily I could try to sleep in Saturday at my house, and Monday, be ready to go again. This was probably day eight of my manic episode and I still had five days left until it broke, but I was enjoying every bit of it while it lasted.

As I sat in Miss Geanette's class, I started having a weird feeling and I saw a bald cat jump onto her shoulder. I was about to say, *Who the hell is that and how did it get here?* Then I told myself, *Don't believe it, Steve, it's not real,* so I went out and got a Coke, sat on the couch, and then went back in and it was gone. I was starting to get familiar with them and know somewhat what was real and what wasn't, but there was a lot I had to learn before I was able to tell what was real from not.

We had a new math teacher named Miss Swanson. I liked her, but she was a little annoying at times. She was good at math, which I liked, because I needed all the help I could get in math—I hated it, but I wanted to learn how to do it correctly. She would sit down with us and give us basically free tutoring. I was hearing voices as well and going through mania, so when she would turn around, I would hear either, *Man, she's got a flat ass,* or *Did you only eat a grape today?* because she was very thin. I started to laugh so hard that I got sent up to the couch to cool off for a bit. They never knew what I was laughing at nor would I ever tell them. She looked like she only weighed about one hundred pounds or less. She was very emaciated, but maybe she had something wrong with her. I didn't know, so I tried not to judge, because I was seriously messed up myself. I'm sure she wasn't having hallucinations like me, but you never know unless you've walk a mile in their shoes, as my mother says. Probably half the people in America say this and it's a good saying that I like.

Some days after school, I would see James, who had turned very religious. It was weird seeing him like that, because I never took him for the religious type, but I guess growing up and going through depression himself, he picked up the Bible and never put it down. That I understand, which is why I never judge him. It's a free country and he has all the right in the world for what he does. I even get a free preaching lesson every now and then. I like hearing about stuff like that, plus, it makes him happy, so I let him preach away. He loved to work out, too so we would get in a quick pump session and then come back and watch Pee Wee Herman. We always had the biggest laugh at that—we could have watched it a thousand times and still laughed every time we saw it.

James made me watch *The Passion of Christ* with him. I liked it, but it was pretty gruesome. I was used to that after watching all my slasher films, so I had to sit through the whole movie. Even though it got very boring, I respected James and kept watching.

I get very nostalgic over these memories, because they are some of the best of my life, especially with Tyler, until I met some more friends and we made some new memories. Tyler and I will always have the best memories though, because we did so much stuff together. He pretty much grew up at my house and I at his. His family is basically my family, but still they didn't know what was going on with me. They probably thought I was on drugs, because when I was manic, my pupils would enlarge into nothing but black.

If I didn't know any better, I would have thought I was on drugs, too. But instead of being high on drugs, I was high from my mania, which is the best high I think you can get, plus, like I said, it's free. All I have to do is wait for it to pop through, but I would never stop my medicine to find out. I knew I was going to be in deep crap, if I did that, so I just had to sit patiently and wait for it to come. While I had it for those two weeks, I was living the dream, little sleep but achieving so much I was a mad man on the run searching for the next adrenaline rush to heighten my senses.

Miss Geanette had to go out one day and I heard her ask Miss Christina to sit in class with us. Miss Christina said, "I will not sit in there with that animal." I started to laugh and went out there laughing in her face and I got an hour's detention after school, but it was worth it, I despised her so much. Instead of that, we had to open the slider that separated rooms, so Mrs. Whitley could watch us.

Shubby and I would always joke around with her, but Shubby was a bit too sexual and embarrassed her. It actually embarrassed me, too, but for some reason, she never said anything to Mrs. Detra. I think she was about to talk to her though, since he never shut up about it. My mania soon went away, but that brought on a deep depression and I was miserable. It took me forever to do my schoolwork and I was very distracted and extremely antisocial. If anyone asked, I would just say I wasn't feeling good at the time.

I would look forward to the days Tyler came over to play *Call of Duty* and go to the mall. This was my favorite game, because we would get into it and Tyler would yell at the screen, which I would laugh at. Even though I was depressed, that always cheered me up. He was very good at it when he got his MoJo—I wished I were as good as he was. We would also play *Call of Duty: Zombies*. When I knew only an hour was left before he had to leave, my depression would hit again and I couldn't shake it, but at least I got to see him for a couple of hours.

He was still in twelfth grade at the time and it was about halfway through the year. That's I met my friend, Dan. We saw each other at SMA, but never talked. He was a good kid and became my very good friend. Finally, when we started to hang out, I was invited to his house, where we went out on his boat in this huge lake behind his house. We would also go to his tree fort and just talk all day while he would have a cigarette or two.

I met some good friends through Dan, and some bad. I would invite some of them over my house, but others I wouldn't let within five hundred feet of it. I won't give any names, but a lot of them were drug addicts and I didn't trust most of them, because my dad had a lot of painkillers for his shoulder, which would be an all you can eat buffet for them to get whatever they wanted. Drug addicts are very smart. They know the generics for medicine and some can even tell what the pill is by the color. I knew a lot about drugs by reading and researching them. Anything that alters your brain chemistry is very bad for you. I still had some good friends that were addicts, but I trusted them a little. It took a while before they got sober, so they could come over to my house.

Dan liked to hang around with a group of friends, but I didn't. I felt very uncomfortable around so many people. I just didn't feel like I fit into society, but I tried to make friends with everyone I saw. I looked up and read what each drug looked like and the high it would give you, because I wanted to be able to tell when one of my friends was high. It wasn't that hard to tell—it was actually quite easy to figure out if they were or not.

Every one of them knew I drove a truck, so I was always their ride. If said no, they would guilt trip me and basically beg me, so I would give in. I would help my friends move, and since I had a truck, I was the go to guy.

The only friends I didn't care about driving around was Tyler and Dan. Tyler would drive me everywhere, so I would even let him drive my truck. I also let Dan drive it, until he was able to give me rides. Tyler and Dan were very good drivers and never drove drunk or high. I respected that so much and thanked them

for not doing anything stupid. Tyler only had one speeding ticket, while Dan didn't have any, but I still trusted Tyler to take my
truck. He never sped in it, because it would put my truck and
our lives in jeopardy. I would have made him pull over and let
me drive, but that wasn't the case with Tyler and Dan. I trusted
them with my life.

We were pulling into Dan's driveway, when I saw a bunch of
sadistic creatures, so I made him stop. I asked if he saw them, but
he said, "Saw what?"

I said "The creatures—can you see them?" so he slowly pulled
in and started to pass the creatures. When I got up to his house,
he asked if I was okay or if I needed to go home, I said, I was
kidding, but he knew I wasn't. He asked me if I wanted to go on
the boat and cool off, so we did. Even though it was dark, the
neighborhood lights and the moon brightened it up. When we
were getting close to his house, I saw a gang of archers ready to
shoot us, so I looked away and closed my eyes. When I looked
back, they were gone, thank God.

Dan also had a dirt bike that was beautiful. He took me for
a ride once and right when we got to the road, he did a wheelie.
It went through this jungle of a yard like it was like a maze, but
it was incredible and so much fun, even though I thought I was
going to die.

I was spending the night once on his futon in his room, while
he was on the bed. I kept hearing noises coming from the kitch-
en, so I went to investigate. When I got there, I saw this evil black
mass standing about twenty feet from me. I was frozen in fear
and didn't know what to do, since I wasn't home. I sort of hurried
back to the futon and covered my eyes. I felt like waking Dan
up, but he wouldn't like that and it would make me seem crazy.
Plus, he was snoring, so he was in a deep sleep. When I went to
the bathroom, he always kept the curtain shut, so I couldn't see
what was behind it. While I was urinating, I heard a growl from
behind the curtain, so without even finishing, I hurried back to

the futon, where I eventually fell asleep. I was so happy when it was daylight, I can't even put it into words.

When Dan and I would go out on the boat in daytime, we would go to an island in the middle of his lake and crawl up onto it. We would walk around trying to find turtle or snake eggs and sometimes we saw a cracked open bird's egg. I'm sure there were alligators in his lake, but we never found any, which was good for us, because I'm deathly afraid of them, but I would rather see an alligator than a snake. We went fishing in his pond and caught a good amount of fish—nothing to brag about it, but I loved it no matter what—we could talk and fish.

Going down Dan's driveway at night is sort of scary. There are palmettos along each side of his yard and finally you get to his house, but it's pitch black at night with not one light, so I would press my keys, making them flash, until I got to my truck. When I was going down his driveway once, I saw a big hairy man-looking thing walking in front of my truck. That made me paranoid, because Dan was already inside. I couldn't go knocking on his door, if nothing was there. I waited it out and finally got the courage to drive out of there alive. Then I was looking in the backseat constantly to make sure there was nothing behind me, which was one of my worst trips home.

I felt like calling Dan and asking if I could sleep over. I had to be a tough guy and make it home, because I knew nothing could get me from the safety of my truck and there was nothing behind me. On my way home, I heard a voice whisper in my ear calling, "Steve, Steve, Steve," over and over again. I wanted to get home so bad, I could hardly stand it, but I was horrified. What made it worse is there weren't any cars on the road and it was pitch black, but when I got to a traffic light then I felt a little better. After hearing that voice, I didn't want to look back, but I had to. I saw nothing behind me, which was a big relief, but I kept hearing my name—just constantly, "Steve, Steve, Steve, …" I had to ignore it the whole ride home.

Finally when I got home, it said, "I will be waiting for you when you get back, Steve." I thought, *Not a chance, asshole, you're not going to control my life.* I quickly went up to the garage door, opened it, and went straight for my room to go to bed and get those hallucinations out of my head.

Mom usually waited up for me, but that night, after all that was happening, she had gone to bed, so I had to wait for the garage door to shut and walk to my room in pitch black, but I had a night light in my room. I knew my dogs were in there waiting for me, so I felt so much safer than I thought I was. I knew if my dogs weren't alert, I was fine, because then I knew it was only me and no one else is here but me and my family and my dogs. My dogs would have been able to protect me anyway. Shelly was old and Peanut was a small fat dog. I was screwed either way, if it was real, but I knew better than that, because I had been going through this for a while. I don't ever think someone can fully get used to hallucinations—they still startle me to this day.

While my mania left for the time being, I was always so tired and sleeping in class, but somehow keeping my grades and my hallucinations stayed. I always wondered why my visuals and auditory didn't just go away, too? I didn't understand that part of this illness—why couldn't the best part stay and the worst part leave, only coming every now and then like my mania?

My hallucinations were trying to make a point—what that was I don't know, but all I knew is it wasn't ever going away, which made me even more paranoid about telling my parents. Maybe they would think I was on LSD or PCP or something like that, but I wasn't. I knew I had a horrible illness. I had been doing a lot of research and came across many different illnesses, but I didn't know what they were at the time. I thought someone had cursed me—I don't know who—but I was for sure I was cursed. The devil had taken my soul and he was waiting for me to join him and put me through eternal misery. I felt like it was true as hell, pardon the pun, but in a way I didn't think so. I would also ask James about the Bible and try to figure out what all of this meant. Was I literally going insane or was it a curse or a test by God that he wanted me to do something for him?

I started to have all these weird thoughts, like I was meant to be someone else that I already was or I was given special powers to rid the world of evil, but I never tried, because I knew they were erroneous beliefs in my head. I had to fight the urging of these voices saying I was no good to this world and that I might as well die. Obviously, I didn't listen to the voices, because I'm still here, but they would startle me—I would always ask what I did wrong and why me? Sometimes they would talk back to me, saying I wasn't good for the world and they would tell me because of all the evil I've done, even though I had done nothing—they were just devilish voices and visions.

One day I was watching *The Ring,* the movie that scared me as a boy. I tried to leave, because I saw the girl starting to come though my TV screen like 3D, but I couldn't move. I was paralyzed with fear at that point, so I closed my eyes and asked God to take this curse away, but when I opened them, she was still there. I ran to the kitchen and got some water, but when I came back she was gone. I told myself no more horror movies before bed and went straight to my room and slept it off.

Grandpa Dick would always call me out on staying up too late, but I was eighteen, so I could go to bed however late I wanted to, because I wasn't a baby anymore—I was a grown kid. I never argued with him though—I just ignored it the best I could, but my temper was starting to rise almost to the point of full-blown rage. I called this bipolar power, because if I was going through rage, I could lift anything and not feel it. It was like having more superhuman powers like in my manic stage, but this was different. It felt great!

A couple of times I was able to test my strength when I was in a rage by working out—I was unstoppable and anything was possible. It was full-on adrenaline, because after my rage was over, I was extremely tired and had no energy. I was lazy the whole next day—it was like coming off mania. I wasn't depressed after my rage, like I was with mania, but I couldn't do a damn thing. I felt like a lazy bum.

I would still try to go to the gym, but it was hard, because my body ached and my mind was mush. I didn't feel like I could go to school when the weekend was up, but my parents forced me to try my hardest. I ended up going home depressed, so I just went back to the park to swing and cool down. Swinging helped my depression and mood, I felt free like my problems were on the ground and couldn't get to me but as soon as my feet hit the ground all my emotions would crawl back up and consume me.

While the baseball field was open, I would walk around the field just for exercise and let go of my mind. Sometimes I would buy a good baseball and throw it against the fence hard enough for it to come back to me and play catch by myself. Sometimes James would meet me at the field or I would pick him up and play ball. Since he was a truant, he was never at school, so every now and then, I would go over, if I were having a bad day.

Then twelfth grade came along and it wasn't until a half a year later, I finally told my parents when I couldn't take it anymore. All my friends were gone either to college or just out of high school. My hallucinations were worse, because I had no friends in twelfth grade, besides a couple of people a grade below me, but I never hung out with them. The good part was that I was still in contact with my friends who graduated, but the only friend I had left in school was Dan, which was a plus, because he was starting to become a good friend of mine. I would still host UFC fights and my friends Dylan, Tyler, Dan, Joe, Shubby, and Cohen Tyler's friend would all come over nights. Everyone would sleep over again, so all we needed was beer, but we were still all underage. My parents would let us order pizza or Chinese and have it delivered to the house. Everyone pitched in to get food, because our fights started. That was a rough night for me, because my hallucinations were nothing but chaos. I couldn't enjoy the fights while seeing fairies flying around everyone and talking in my ears. I just went to the bathroom and took a Tylenol. When I got back, they were all gone, so I went back into the bathroom, washed my face, but when I came back out and all of them were there again.

In twelfth grade, I decided that I wanted to graduate early, so I took a lot of time after school doing homework and extra class to achieve my goal. It was tough though, because it was so much work in such a little amount of time, but I loved it. I loved the cadence—I would still hear my name being called, but I knew it was a hallucination. I still checked anyway, just in case it was a real person calling me, but it never was though.

My math teacher at the time, Miss Swanson, was also tutoring me and she was very good at it. She was almost a math genius—how she could come up with the answer right away without a calculator baffled me. I would go home and go over my reading and math. I would use my white board to practice all my multiplication and division. I studied my numbers and got pretty good at it, but sometimes I needed to use a calculator. I'm the type of person who needs to be perfect in what I'm doing or I feel obsolete. I always have to be one step ahead, so I tried to make sure I was the best at anything I did, no matter what, but it seemed like the only thing I was good at was hallucinating.

I would spend all day in my room studying everything I could about mental illness, but was stuck on bipolarity. I would read as much as I could about it and take notes on what I was reading, but I didn't know where the hallucinations fit in. Most say mania is the cause of it, but I was hallucinating without any episodes of mania. I was very depressed at the time and had been for quite some time, since I was coming down from my two-week mania high, I was reading and writing as much as I could about any mental illness I came across.

Finally one day, my mom sat me down and started asking questions. One question I will never forget is, "Are you depressed?" I had been caught. I wish I would have said no, but I had to tell the truth about it.

At the time, she didn't know I was hallucinating, because I kept that to myself for the time being. Now my task was done—I had graduated high school. I was so relieved that I was able to do it with all these problems I was having.

Working at the Dog Pound

DURING THE SUMMER, I GOT A JOB WORKING AT THE dog pound cleaning up after the puppies. The best part is, I had the whole twelve kennels to myself. I could work at my own pace and walk as many dogs as I could. I was cleaning out the kennels once and saw a large pale white man walk by. Since I was by myself, I freaked out and didn't want to go back into the kennel the whole day. I went into the break room and read my books, but I walked into the kennel every fifteen minutes to make sure it was clean, so I was doing my job, but it was very hard to keep up with it.

No matter how much suffering I was going through, I loved all the dogs. It made me happy to take them out and play with them. I would take extra time cleaning their kennels, because they deserved to live in a fresh clean kennel. A clean kennel is a happy dog. I would take them to the yard to play in a fenced lot, after they did their business. Then I would wash them, so when families would check them out, their nice fur coats smelled fresh and clean. I worked in the quarantine area where the dogs went when they first got to the pound to make sure that they didn't have ticks, worms, or any diseases before they went into general population.

I only worked on weekends, so one Saturday, while I was cleaning a kennel, the door shut and locked me in. Then I heard a very dark demented voice say, "They are mine now and I'm going to kill every one of them," so I quickly climbed the wall and made it out okay. Luckily, I was under two hundred pounds or I would have broken it, but those dogs were my priority and they would never be hurt on my watch.

The thing about my voices is they seem so real that it's hard to distinguish what's real from what's not. It's like someone is literally speaking into my ear—I go into a trance-like state.

The best part about working in quarantine is the puppies are also my responsibility. They make such a mess though, but they can't help it—they are just babies. It took me a good hour to clean their kennels, plus, they all had worms, so I had to wear a full protective suit, so I didn't spread it.

The smell was so horrible, I would open the back gate where it was fenced in and let them run and play as long as they wanted. I would get into trouble for having them out, so I just said, "They're babies, so they need to be outside. I made sure I cleaned the area they were in, so I didn't contaminate anything.

No puppy wants to grow into an adult without ever seeing the sun, so I just let them play in the sun as long as I could. The gates were shut and they had a perfect place to run around in, after I cleaned their kennels. I kept them out a little longer for the kennel to dry. Four kennels were for the puppies and two were full of about three puppies to a kennel. I heard a weird noise and turned around to see a man with no face—just a sunken-in face with no eyes or nose. I stared at it for a couple minutes, which felt like a lifetime, and it said, "They're my family now."

I knew that quote was from a horror movie I had watched, but he was not going to get my puppies! I thought it would be fun to spray the hose at my hallucination, just for the hell of it, but it just went straight through it. That was a relief, because then I knew it was safe to continue my work.

On Saturday, I worked eight till five and Sundays, from eight till eleven. Saturdays were hectic, because that's when dogs were being shown to potential buyers to give them a home, but I had nothing to worry about. I was in my own pod all by myself. I saw the dogs in a different way—I viewed them as family, because no dog wants to be locked up for life, so I would pet them and hold them as much as possible and clean their cage right when they did their business.

I was hallucinating the whole time I was there, so just everywhere I went, I would see ghosts, demons, or something demonic. I knew it was because of all the horror movies I used to watch, so I knew I had it coming for me sooner or later.

I still watched them though—it was fascinating to me. I didn't like the gory films—just the suspense thriller. Yes, they was still murdering people, but it wasn't like real gore. I thought, *What the hell, it can't make things worse,* but it did. I was just adding fuel to the fire.

On nights during the week, I would stay at Tyler's, because he had graduated, too. We would watch horror movies all damn night. I felt safe with him in the room with me, but I still heard my name being called out and I would see angels flying by me. I thought the light for sure would wake Tyler up, but it didn't. Then they flew by again singing, which actually put me to sleep. Was it real or just a coincidence? I wanted it to be real, to show me that there is a God, but it was just my hallucinations kicking back in.

The next Saturday, I was back working my butt off. The dogs were always so excited to see me. I could tell by the smiles and knowing I would extend their playtime—the same as with the puppies. After cleaning extra kennels to kill time for them to be outside and to make sure it was squeaky clean for when they came back in, my mood was starting to fall. Nothing made me happy anymore, because when I was manic, not even the dogs made me happy.

I would go home straight to my room, shut and lock the door, and read and study brain diseases and mental illness. My mom knew I was depressed, but I told my parents nothing else at that time. I wanted to keep it like that, because how would I explain to my family that I was having visual and auditory hallucinations? I didn't know how to say or how to put it without them thinking I was on drugs. However, they could have tested me to make sure, but I was an idiot.

Maybe if I had told someone earlier—like my mom—I could have gotten help quicker and diminished the problems I was having. I knew it would never be cured, but I had to try on my own before my parents became involved. I would always bring a book in on Saturdays, so when I finished my work, I could read. I had been doing that for a while, but then my boss caught me and told me to stop or he would put a demerit on my record. At this point, I didn't care if I got fired or not. I knew I would be able to get a better job with better pay, so I wasn't worried about that.

I had delusional thinking that all the dogs could read my mind and I could read theirs. I would ask if they had to go pee and they would say, "Yes, Steve." I remember how cool I felt that I had that power. I felt literally like Dr. Doolittle, except only with dogs. I knew it sounded crazy, but I could hear them talking to me. I could hear them saying, "Let me out of this kennel."

"I'm going crazy," I would reply back. "I can't or I will get into trouble."

Instead I brought them to the yard and played for a bit. I also got in trouble for that, because I wasn't allowed to give them too much time out. I didn't care—these dogs wanted out, so they were going to get out. I just asked my boss, "How would you feel if you were stuck in a cage all day with no sunlight and having to walk about in your own feces?"

She agreed to that and they were allowed extra time in the yard, but only pod three could get the special big yard, because of the worry about worms. The dogs that had bacteria or viruses were led to this concrete yard, which was easily washed. One of my favorite dogs there had a fatal disease and had to be euthanized, so before she was put down, I sat and talked with her a bit, telling her it will be okay and that there is a better place for you. Then my time was up and she was put to sleep. She never deserved to be put to sleep, but she was in pain or I hope she was, so it would have been worth it for her to go to sleep forever. She was dying anyhow, so it was for the best.

Sometimes when I would clean their kennel, I would listen to music in my head with no earplugs or anything. Suddenly, inside my head I heard a loud roar. When I came out of the kennel, I was staring into the eyes of a massive T-Rex. When I ran outside, it followed me out the door, but when I got outside and quickly looked back, the beast was gone. I was still afraid to go in there after that, but I had to do my job, so I was on high alert the whole day. I would also see raptors running towards me at high speed, but at this point, I walked outside instead of running, because I knew it was fake. I just couldn't go into that pod for the time being.

I would be cleaning the kennel and see shadows running behind me, so I would look around thinking it was another employee, but saw no trace of anyone ever going in there, plus, I would have heard the door open or close. I thought, *How the hell is this possible? Only something with solid mass could create a shadow like that.* It was too tall to be an animal and almost too tall to be a human. It would have to be something demonic, but how could I tell if it was or not? I had seen angels and demons, but I only wished the angels were real. If the demons were real, then that means there is a higher power out there somewhere, but why am I just seeing and hearing demonic entities? It helps me get through, knowing there has to be a God and whenever I would pray for my hallucinations to go away, most of the time they were answered, but sometimes the demonic entities would linger for quite some time. As I said before, I was never the religious type and neither was James, until he turned all of a sudden. I believe I was given this illness for a reason—to help people like me find the light at the end of the tunnel.

I was making less than two hundred bucks a paycheck, but that was a lot of money to me. I had never had a job before and I bought the American Psychiatric Association, DSM4TR, which is a book full of mental illnesses. It was one hundred and fifty bucks, but I loved it. I read as much as I could. I brought that to work with me sometimes hoping I would get fired then that would be my breaking point to tell my family what was wrong with me.

They liked me there though and they even told me so. I tried my best to fit in, but I did not like my second boss in command—she was a rude, fat, mean person. I wasn't afraid to tell her off, if it came to that, because I wanted to get fired, but I had to come up with a nifty plan to get fired, but I never pulled it off. I worked there for a while and tried to like my job as much as I could. I would just tell myself that these dogs needed me. If I left, who would give them extra playtime in the yards or clean up their kennel as good as me, so I stuck with it for a while.

Sometimes there would be dogs tied to the tree out front when people for some reason didn't want their dogs. It was sad to see, but they were given a good home. Not one dog was mean, although there was this dog named Elizabeth, that would nip at people and bite her leash. She had some type of neuro-logical defect, so we had to euthanize her. It was sad, but she was too mean to try to handle. She only let me pet her. I was cautious, so she was nice to me.

Every time I was cleaning kennels, no matter what my mood was, I would always have hallucinations in the pod I was in. I saw a bloodied dead dog walking towards me and I thought it was revenge for her being put down, but I ignored it and went on with my business.

My hallucinations were starting to get worse. It was happen-ing everywhere—even in places I knew were safe. Even during the week, I would spend all my time in my room, reading and studying. My mom could tell something horrible was wrong and kept asking me if I was depressed, so I would say yes.

The final straw is when I started not to want to go work, no matter how much I loved it. I was a strong kid, but the hallucinations were starting to get the best of me and they were happening all day and night. Shadow people, demons, angels, Jesus, God, bodies hanging from the walls, and people hanging from the ceiling with nooses around their necks. Chucky was in my closet and starting to walk out after me—you name it—I've pretty much seen it.

While I was cleaning kennels, I could see dark thunderclouds starting to form and rain, but I wasn't getting wet, so I knew what it was, and it was lightning inside the pod I was working in. When that was over with, I went in back to get dog food and I saw three girls playing jump rope right where I was supposed to get the food. I went back out and asked for it to be gone and I ran in there, got the food, and got the hell out, but this was a couple of months *before* I broke it to my mom and dad.

Even though I just worked weekends, I was so depressed and having so many hallucinations, I didn't want to go in. When I did, I would finish up the quickest scrubbing of their whole kennel, rinsing it off, and drying it. Then I would go to the break room and read—like I said, I was basically trying to get fired without being too obvious. I received another warning—she said she doesn't want to see me in the break room anymore.

The next Saturday when I was done working, I went straight back into the break room, sat on the couch, and read my book on bipolarity. I knew sooner or later someone would snitch on me and then when that happened, she would fire me without me having to quit. Even while reading, I couldn't get rid of the hallucinations. They followed me everywhere, so I thought if I tried to hide, maybe they couldn't find me. That was stupid of me, because it's in my head, so no matter where I could run or hide, they would always be there.

The only time I was on my best behavior is when I was cleaning the kennels, because the dogs looked forward to being in a nice clean cage and that was my responsibility. I was taking them to the yard to play, since that's the only thing my dogs looked forward to—getting out of quarantine and having a family adopt them. I saw many dogs get adopted while I was there, some fresh out of my pod right when they were safe to go into population. I was going to miss them, but I was happy to see them go. My depression sort of lifted when I saw that, because I love seeing animals happy.

On Saturdays when we were there until five, the dinnertime was at four and they loved hearing that food cart ride by. It was almost like Pavlov's dogs—when they heard it, they would run to the inside kennel and get their food. I didn't tell anyone, but while I was cleaning, I would let some of the dogs out on my side to come out and play in the pod. If they pooped, I would clean it up and the same if they peed.

The kennel had two separated sides, the inside and outside, with a lever that would trap them on either side. If they went out to the outside kennel, I would pull the lever blocking them, so I could clean the inside and then when the inside was clean, I would switch places and bring them indoors, so I could clean outdoors. I probably should not have done this, but while I cleaned the puppies that weren't in the puppy room and in my pod, I would let them wander around in my pod. If I heard someone coming down the hallway, I would quickly gather them up and put them in their kennel. I could tell they were having the time of their life and I didn't want them to grow up behind a damn cage—I wanted them to explore and get used to the big world they live in.

When I finished scrubbing their kennel, I would sit outside on the ground playing with them—they were so cute. Sometimes even if I was done cleaning, I would let them roam some more in my pod, which was a huge area for them to check out, if they didn't have anything else to do. I would sneak them snacks every now and then, before they got their puppy chow.

In my pod there was a huge Rottweiler named Kaity, who had been beaten her whole life. she was in my pod, because she had worms. I would take care of her and pet her. Although I never trusted her, I knew I could pet her through the cage. Finally she was out and got adopted right away, but about a week later, she was back in my pod. She had bitten a kid, but was probably provoked. She had to be put down and I hated that, because she was such a sweet dog—she didn't deserve to die. All I can say is she is in doggy heaven enjoying herself with her family at her side.

In my pod in the very back room is where the freezer was for all the dead animals, cats included. I would check it every now and then, but they were all stuffed into garbage bags—what a 'great' idea—being put in a damn trash bag. The next day, which was a Sunday, I saw Katie standing in front of me. She had her fur back and didn't look like she had one mark on her, she was so beautiful. She started to walk up to me, so I put my hand out to pet her, but my hand went right through her, which is what I had expected to happen. I don't even know why I put my hand out in the first place, but maybe it was a sign, since I had treated her so well and she wanted to let me know she was in a good place. It was almost as if she were saying her final goodbye before she went to Paradise and then I never saw her again.

That's where my hallucinations get a little too real, because how could I have known if that was real or not, because it seemed so real, I couldn't tell. Was it the spirit of Katie? I didn't know, but for the next month, I tried my best to come up with a good speech to tell my parents what had and has been going on, but I couldn't help but want to die before I told them I was having all these problems. I would not want them to have to explain that their only son was insane.

My work was starting to get hurt by it, too. I was tired and lethargic and had no drive to do anything, so I would just sit in the break room, waiting for the boss to come in. It wasn't a smart way to handle the situation, but I didn't care—I just wanted to be gone, but she never fired me. She would just give me a warning. I kept thinking about what's a nice way to get fired without seeming so anxious to get fired, but I didn't want to upset my parents by doing something stupid, but I did every possible thing I could do to get fired that didn't jeopardize my next job I were to get another one. They would always tell me what a good person I was and at that point, I knew I wasn't going to get fired.

My voices were getting to the point to where I could see a person's lips moving, but all I heard were my voices. Then an hour after they left, they would come in and say, "Did you get it done?" I was like, "I'm sorry I forgot! Could you tell me again?" I could tell they would get frustrated with me and probably thought I was ignoring them completely. Sometimes I would go into the break room and just listen to my voices to give me company and if no one was around, I would talk to them here and there.

Some days if I wanted to get really deep into a conversation with myself, I would act like I was on the phone, so I wasn't being so obvious about it. I could carry on conversations and talk and talk and then when I was done, I would act like I was hanging up the phone. No one asked a single question, so now I knew what I had to do, if I wanted to talk to myself.

I always thought it was funny when the boss would say, "Get back to work," and I would reply, "I'm finished and I was just making my rounds." She always says, "Make yourself useful," but right after saying that I would see her smoking with other employees. I felt like saying, "I smoke, too, so could I get some peace and quiet until it's time for my other patrol of the puppies and dogs?"

I had my work cut out for me with the puppies, but I didn't care—they were my babies. I was also in charge of bathing them, but they were easy, because they didn't fight like most of the dogs did. They were a pain in the butt to wash though, because the puppies are so messy. I just had to wear my outfit and not spread the germs and especially, not bring it home and contaminate my dogs.

I was very careful with these puppies, so they could go through my pod and into population to get adopted and have great lives like dogs should. Sometimes I would get to work early to find a box in front of the gate with a puppy in it. Usually pit bulls were dropped off, but there were also normal puppies in crates. They would go straight to the puppy room to be examined by the vet and get them ready to go through my pod. After that, they were good to go up for adoption.

One day, I walked into the puppy room and saw all the puppies off their cots and lying dead on the floor, so I opened up the door to let sunlight in. I heard them panting from their kennel, so I went back to see their happy faces waiting to go outside, because their kennel was absolutely filthy. They had been in their dirty kennel all night with nowhere to go to do their business, so it was my duty to take care of them. It seemed like every time I washed them, blood would come out of the faucet and stain them, but I turned it off and back on again. It was still there, so I turned it off for a couple more minutes with the puppy still in the tub and when I turned it back on, it was all gone.

It wasn't fair that the smokers were allowed a break every ten minutes, for a five-minute break. I should have started smoking to get that ability. I was always complimented on how clean my pod kennels were, because I kept up with it and I didn't let any poop or pee sit there over five minutes or the puppies would catch another virus that they didn't have before.

Wednesdays were supposed to be deep clean days using dish soap and scrubbing all over the place, but I would do that every Saturday, too. I was there to make sure they were extra clean, but I would get in trouble for using the dish soap on non-deep cleaning days, but I didn't care—all I wanted was to have my dogs lay or sit in a fresh clean kennel that smelled very good. Even on Sundays, when all we are supposed to do is mop, I would get the soap sprayer and deep clean their kennels again and scrub down the puppy kennels. If they complained, I would say, "Would you want to sit in your own feces?" They wouldn't have anything to say to that.

Even though how I did so much extra, I never felt appreciated for all I was doing for the dogs—extra time outside, their food on time, showers when needed, and deep scrubbing their kennels. Whenever I would go into the break room to read about mental illnesses, the boss would walk in. It made me seem like I was sitting down on the job, so I would say, "Go check the kennels and smell in there." When she did, after she got back she said, "Thanks," so I knew I had pleased and impressed her. I would even spray the outside of their kennels on the concrete, because since they had worms, they had to be specially cleaned so they would be adopted.

I was walking on the outside with my house and I heard a growl. When I turned around, I saw a massive dog on its hind haunches ready to attack, so I sprayed it. The water went straight through its body, so I just kept cleaning my kennels. It was staring at me the whole time, just ready to attack, and it was bigger than Cujo.

Picking up the poop while carrying a trashcan with me was brutal, because on a hot day, the smell of putting poop in a hot trash bin was just horrible. When that was done, then came the D64, I think it was called, fresh soap that smelled amazing A huge barrel of it was in the kitchen where we prepared the dogs' food. Some dogs were on special diets, if they were too emaciated or required worm diets, while some were just good dogs and were treated extra special. I didn't believe in that, because all the dogs were special to me, especially in my pod, so I would give all of them treats every now and then.

One day, I went to feed the puppies and when I opened their

kennel, I saw blood everywhere, covering the walls and bottom of their cage. I fed the rest of the dogs, knowing it was just a hallucination. When I was finished with the other dogs, I went back to the puppy kennel and saw that their happy faces were ready for food—they looked so cute as I watched them eat, trying to push each other out of the way to get food. I hate seeing visuals like that, because I never want to see dogs hurt or bloodied, especially when I can't help them.

Everyone there had to wear uniforms, except me. I could wear anything I wanted, because I never had to see anyone. Pod three dogs are not shown until they are safe to go into the population.

I loved my job there, but I still wanted to be fired, so I could go home and face these fears on my own, but nothing I did got me fired. They had a vending machine with Cokes, Pepsi, Dr. Pepper, Sprite and more and I was always raiding the hell out of it. They even had Gatorade, which I always got, because I was trying to watch my weight. I would probably drink three bottles in an eight-hour shift, which doesn't seem much, but they were big bottles.

I visited the water fountain a lot and would get in trouble for using the bathroom so much. I felt like saying, "It's just meth—it helps me focus." That would have been an automatic firing right then and there, but I didn't. I just kept my mouth shut, hoping the cops would become involved, and I didn't want that to happen.

Then it finally happened again—my mania was back. I was so excited to have it back, because I knew I could get so much more work done when I'm like that. The only problem is, I finished so fast and I had nothing else to do all day, but I couldn't help the other employees with dogs, because I had just come from quarantine and might contaminate other dogs. I would just walk the hallways and around my pod to see if they made a mess or not.

I could get so much done it was just incredible! I was flying high again, with nothing to stop me and nothing to get in my way. Even though we were supposed to feed the dogs at four, I would feed them a half hour early so they weren't starving. The next breakfast they were probably hungry as hell, but when I worked Saturdays, I would get there early on Sundays to feed them. I turned on water for the dogs that could reach it, while the others had a bowl.

All week, I was manic, so I was edging the driveway and sweeping, dusting, and sweeping the gym. I thought I was a superhero and I wished for it never to end, but the lack of sleep was going to take a toll on me—I knew that much. I would drink an enormous amount of coffee, just to keep this high going for as long as I could. I didn't need coffee though, since I was as high as could be from this amazing mania.

This happened a week before I broke it to my parents. I was going to wait until the mania went away. I was cleaning using the deep scrubbing machine and finishing all the kennels within three hours, which was basically a record time. So what did I do next? I went straight to the break room and ran into my boss, Lisa. She said there is no way I cleaned those kennels so fast, so I brought her in and showed her. She was amazed. I told her I was keeping my eye on them, so in case they pooped or peed, I was right there to clean it up before they walked in it.

Only when I was manic could I do all that in record time. I could tell some of the staff were jealous of me, because they took so long to do theirs, while I had already finished and was taking the dogs out to their yards. I would let each one stay in the yard for a half hour to forty-five minutes, since it was an eight-hour shift. I thought they deserved more than just fifteen minutes. I would also bring the pooper-scooper and a trash bag to pick up after them. Those dogs were like family to me.

Some Saturdays, I would arrive to a messy kennel with feces even on the walls. I wish I could have known who left it like that, even though it was overnight, they still shouldn't have been that messy. On Saturdays, after I cleaned their kennels, when I came on Sunday, there would be limited feces and urine, because I had cleaned so well the night before. All of it came so easy, while I was manic. I felt like I was floating or swimming—just hovering over their kennels and flying through my work as fast as I could. Then I would have nothing to do the last seven hours, so I would just let them play in the back room as much as they wanted and after they had all been out, I would scrub where they had been, so I didn't pass worms or viruses.

I always looked forward to being done, so I could get a Coke or read. Then my boss, Lisa, would give me another warning for being in there for so long. I had hoped she was going to fire me. I thought it would be easier than having to put in a two-weeks' notice.

Just as fast as it came, the mania left. Deep depression made me tired, lethargic, and lazy—I just couldn't go on anymore. After talking with my mom, I finally put in my two-weeks' notice, which was only four more days of work. I was going to miss the dogs, but not the employees, because they didn't have any respect.

Researching My Mania

I WOULD SPEND HOURS IN MY ROOM READING AND DO-ing research, trying to figure out what was wrong with me. One day, my parents sat me down and asked what was wrong. I couldn't hide it anymore. I said I was depressed and having hallucinations. It must have felt horrible for them knowing I had a mental illness, but we just didn't know what kind. I also told them about my mania, which they knew right then and there, it had to be bipolar, but that didn't explain the hallucinations. People with bipolarity do sometimes hallucinate, but not as much as I was. I said I was seeing shadow figures, but I didn't tell them the gruesome parts of blood or anything like that. I also had to tell them I was hearing evil voices, although perhaps at that time, I just called them voices—not evil ones.

The next couple of days, my mom worked her ass off trying to find a good doctor—the best one she could find. We ran across a doctor named Hakala and had a Skype session on the computer. I explained what was wrong and she prescribed me Xanax, until I had my appointment with her to try to calm my nerves.

That worked for the time being, but that's not the medicine I needed to be on. When she got back into town, I finally got to meet her. She was pretty and very sweet. I remember telling her that I thought I was manic-depressive and she said, "Well, we don't call it that anymore."

I felt like saying, "No shit, lady," but I kept my cool. She also said the voices in my head were thought voices. I told her it's like people talking directly to me, but she didn't listen to me—not one bit. She was always asking us to use herbal remedies, but, of course, that didn't work. We gave it about three days and stopped, because it was ridiculous—that wasn't the answer to my illness.

Next, she prescribed Zoloft, which threw me into a deep bout of psychosis. I think this was the first hospital visit I'd ever gone through and it was on my 19th birthday, which made me even more upset. I remember going in there, but for what, I didn't know, but all I remember is laying on the hospital bed and getting injected with Haldol and Ativan.

The next thing I remember is waking up and being walked out to the police car to transport me to Bayside. When it wore off, I remember crying all night, because I wanted to go home, because I didn't feel safe. It was hard to see my parents, because I knew they were going home without me. After they left, I would never leave my bed, unless the doctor came to see me. I would sleep all day, because I was so heavily medicated, but I always looked forward to seeing the doctor. When he saw me the last time, I heard the words of an angel saying, "You're good to go home."

I called my parents right away and said I was being discharged. They were as excited as I was. I liked the structure there, with meds always a couple hours before bed, so we weren't a bunch of walking zombies. They had me on Seroquel to help me sleep and try to break the hallucinations. I think they also had me on Depakote for a mood stabilizer.

Back then, my diagnosis was bipolar with psychosis. I knew that wasn't right, because I had researched it and those symptoms didn't add up to what I was going through. I was hallucinating without my mania but usually bipolar psychosis happened when you *were* manic.

State College of Florida (SCF)

ABOUT A YEAR AFTER GRADUATION, I THOUGHT IT would be a good idea to go to a community college. I entered one called SCF, because I wanted to go into criminal law, which sounded like a perfect career for me. I took a criminal justice class. The instructor, Greg, was a good guy and very smart. He had been a cop, but was retired.

I loved his class and looked forward to going every day I had a class scheduled. About a week into class, I started to hallucinate bad and I thought, *Christ, why me and why in my favorite class?* I wasn't manic—just a little depressed, but that's about it. Instructor Greg would grow wings and start to levitate, which was pretty damn funny in my opinion. The situation wasn't funny though, because I had to pay close attention in his class, since he would go quite fast. Sometimes it was hard to keep up with him, especially with the voices I was hearing that were talking over his voice.

I looked forward to weekends, because I would go either to Tyler or Dan's house. I was on Depakote at the time. We were walking back from Dan's fort and all I remember is walking. The next thing I knew is that I was in hell—I was yelling that I wanted my old life back and I didn't want to go just yet. In a way, I wasn't afraid. I thought that if it's time to go, then it's time to go. I woke up to Dan patting me on the shoulder and I was laying on my back staring at the trees. His mother came out to check me and it was either call my parents or she was going to call the paramedics, so I called my parents. Within ten minutes, they were there even though we lived a half hour away.

I never had an episode like that with Tyler, although some nights were worse than others. I would wake up in the middle of Tyler's kitchen wearing only my briefs. How I got there I don't know, but I quickly went back to sleep in his room. I didn't have a spare bed to sleep on, so I bunked in with him and that alone made me feel safe and that feeling is in my best interest. I was heavily medicated at the time, so I could hardly walk. Grandpa Dick would sometimes drop me off and pick me up in college. How I made it through criminal justice is a miracle. Even though I was medicated, I was still having problems and a lot of them. My morning meds should have been my night meds, because it would make me so tired and lazy, some days I had to skip class, which I hated doing, because I loved his class so much.

Along with criminal justice, I was also taking math. Those two classes, while heavily medicated, were hard as hell to do, but somehow I did it. Math is hard enough to do, and being so out of it and still having hallucinations made it worse, I was trapped in hell. My voices in math were worse, because I was stressed and it was so quiet in there, I could hear and make out all my voices that were talking. It happened in instructor Greg's class, too, only I could pick out only some words, but it was talking over his damn voice. It's hard to tell in which class my hallucinations were worse, but I would have to say, math. I would see colonies of ants walking by and cockroaches on the walls and then the teacher would turn around. There was feces all over the math instructor.

At this time, I was officially diagnosed manic depressive "bipolar" with psychosis. I took the math teacher aside and told him what I had and how I was trying to work through it, so he gave me a break. If I promised to give him a couple hours a week to tutor me, one-on-one, which was a godsend. I didn't tell him about my hallucinations, even though I should have, but I didn't want to make matters worse.

Once when he was tutoring me, I saw a snake on his neck just sitting there and that sort of frightened me, because I hate snakes. I tried my best to follow him and what he was saying, but I kept hearing a voice telling me that I needed to go. I didn't listen, because I knew I was safe with him in the class with me. It wasn't a crowed class—probably nine students including me and I liked small classes. I felt I could try to concentrate better, even with my problems following me.

In instructor Greg's class, there were probably twenty six people, including me, but I didn't like big classes like that. I would bring in my computer on the days before the big test, because he would blurt out the questions and I couldn't keep up, especially with my voices the way they were. I would have to go up after class and ask him to reiterate what he said. He never acted annoyed or mad, but he just sat me down and we would go through the questions.

I didn't tell him what I had, because I didn't know how he would react. The only person I ever told what I had was my math teacher, because I needed all the support I could get in math. I was in intermediate algebra for not testing too well on my test to get into college, but I didn't care, because I looked at it as a challenge for me to see how much I could go through, even with my hallucinations. I thought maybe if my brain is busy, it would mute my problems, but it only exasperated the situation. I didn't care about my math grade, as much as my criminal justice grade, because I didn't care about math—only criminal justice.

The first test we ever took in criminal justice, I made my own study guide for the test. The next day I took the test and the day after that, they posted our scores—amazingly, I scored a 90%. Halfway through his class after I found out my score, I heard what sounded like a rusty door or gate being opened and closed. It was so damn loud, I had to get the hell out of there saying I had a doctor's appointment. When I got outside, I saw a naked lady pointing at something. When I turned around, I saw what must of been ten people hanging from nooses off tall branches. The lady was old, maybe in her seventies, with wrinkly skin pale as could be, but I can still picture her to this day. It's very haunting to see a visual like that. I didn't care about the people hanging—all I cared about is getting that image out of my head. Nobody wants to see a pale naked old lady—at least I don't—not as young as I was. The next day when I went into criminal justice, I was about a quarter of the way up to the door, when I saw a large wolf, like a werewolf, opening up the door and sticking his head through. I ducked into another building and got a drink. When I entered his class, no one was there except the werewolf. I went back outside to the bathroom and washed my face, got another drink, and went back. This time, the students were there and so was instructor Greg.

Little did I know that what was happening in math and criminal justice was just the beginning. In math, I saw the naked lady again. This time she was standing in the corner crying. I wanted to talk to her, but I would be thrown out for being insane, so that wasn't an option for me, because I knew I needed this class to move on. I liked the saying, "Face your fears," but how was I to face them if they weren't really there? She was there for a good portion of the class, just crying in the corner. I couldn't take my eyes off her, but I couldn't mute the crying.

Ever since I got this disease, I have become an introvert, just wanting to be by myself, listen to my voices, and accept the fate that I was going to be like this for the rest of my life. The day I saw the werewolf in instructor Greg's class, I told myself I would never go through that door again, so I would always take the long way to class through the double door and up the stairs. There were about ten rows of seats in his class. I sat in the very back of this stadium seating, so I could see and hear him better.

One time, I brought a tape recorder, but only once, because he got on a student's ass for bringing a recorder. I was always paranoid that my voices were going to show up on my recorder—that's how real they felt to me.

In instructor Greg's class, I saw the naked lady again, but this time she was pointing right at me. I asked my friend next to me if he could copy some notes for me, because I had to go to a doctor's appointment. He agreed and kindly took notes for me. On the way home from school, I saw her sitting in my back seat. I drove to a gas station, got a monster energy drink, and chugged it. When I went back to my car, she was still there. I thought, *Screw it, if she attacks me, there is nothing I can do about it.* So I faced my fears and got in the truck and tried my best not to look in the rear mirror. I thought to myself, *It's only a hallucination, that's all it is. It'll go away soon, so all I need to do is get home and relax.* When I got home from instructor Greg's class and was walking up to my door, I saw her again. I was so enraged that I went up to punch her and my hand went straight through her. I knew it would, but I was just pissed that she wouldn't leave me alone. I would try to talk to her and sometimes she would talk back. I know it sounds insane, but I am insane, so I didn't think twice about it. She never talked back, but none of mine talked back until later, but I'll get to that part.

I had names for some of my people I would see, but I forgot them, so I'll call the naked lady, Diane. Even if I would address her by name when I called her, she would never answer back. Diane followed me everywhere, but it was good company—just shows how messed up my disease is to have a name for my hallucination. I was also having voices while seeing Diane, and at night, my voices would address me by name saying, "They just want to visit." I would say, "No, I'm trying to sleep." Then I would hear scratching on the wall and demonic growls like I had heard before.

One night, I heard a noise in my closet and turned to open it. Before I could move, I saw the doorknob slowly start to turn and start to open. I jumped into my bed, turned my light on, and watched the knob almost all night long. Then the next morning, I had to hear from Grandpa Dick who asked, "Why was your light on all night?" I told him I was reading a book.

Little did anyone know I was hallucinating, even though I had told my parents some of my issues, I didn't tell them all the problems I was having. I still thought they would throw me into an asylum for the rest of my life. That is a fear that still grips me to this day. I would die if I had to be locked in an asylum.

The next day, when I was back in instructor Greg's class, he didn't even know I had left, but I got the notes from my friend and copied them into my notes. That was a life saver, because we had a pop quiz the next day and I scored a 92%. After the quiz, I heard the loud rusty metal gate start to open and close—it got so loud, I couldn't hear a thing and that pissed me off. I was about to stand up and scream, "Who the hell is doing that?" I would have most likely been sent to the office to cool down and get a grip on myself, but then my whole class would think I'm a psycho, so I held back as much as I could.

I was passing all my criminal justice exams with A's, because I made such a good system to study and my mom would read them out to me and I would answer. Bringing my computer helped me to keep up with his questions. I wish I had done it sooner, but I learned by my mistakes. Luckily, I had an amazing buddy to help me with the questions when I didn't bring my computer. It was easy to take notes in his class, especially with my computer, plus, he would have us highlight certain parts that were going to be on the test. I took as much help as possible and took notes and highlighted what he told us to highlight. Since he was an ex-cop, he knew a lot of stuff—almost everything you need to know and he was just an all-around amazing instructor. I was in his class and put my head down. When I looked back up, all the students had their heads down and were bleeding, so I thought, *Oh God, here we go again.* I went to the hallway to get a drink and when I came back, everything was back to normal.

The good thing was that it was test day, so we got to go home early. I breezed through my test, knowing I knew it all and left without looking back. When I got to my truck, Diane, the naked lady, was standing next to my door, almost as if she were trying to block me from getting in. I didn't care at this point. I was just so tired and wanted to get home and wait for my dad to work out. I walked right past her and heard a scream. I knew it was her, so I never even thought of looking back. The rest of the ride home was hell. I could hear her horrible screams in the back seat. I kept looking back to see if I could see her, but I couldn't, I could only hear the screams. I would hear Diane saying that I needed to turn back, because my home wasn't safe, but I knew it was safe, so I kept driving and was relieved to get to my safe home without listening to her.

Even though I was on meds the whole time, we needed a new game plan, because what I was taking wasn't helping me at all. I was still with my first psychiatrist at this point and my parents hadn't switched me my new doctor, who is still my doctor to this day. Vitamins and herbal remedies were her approach to my illness, but that never worked either. She was a great doctor, but not the right doctor for me. She would also have me do these stupid workbook worksheets, trying to find my inner self. Those didn't work either, because my hallucinations were so bad, nothing except medicine could help me. I tried to tell her that, but she said let the remedies do their work and I couldn't wait that long—not with all these problems happening.

I felt like my mind was slowly starting to fade into blackness, I needed true meds. All she ever prescribed was Xanax and Zoloft and we already know what Zoloft did to me. While I was seeing her, things got worse. I would see Diane everywhere—even in the bathroom and that was pretty close for my comfort. She was probably seven feet away from me, but when I would shower, I would see her in the bathtub with the tub completely full. She said I should take kava kava for anxiety, but it didn't work. It's bad for the liver, so I stopped taking that right away, plus, it made me paranoid about my well-being. I like my liver and wanted to keep it where it is. Sometimes herbal remedies aren't as safe as prescriptions. Some drugs don't hurt the body as much as herbal medicine. It's like star fruit—very good for you, but very bad for you—mainly the kidneys.

The next day, I had criminal justice, which I had three times a week. I tried to get both math and criminal justice on the same day, so I didn't have to ride to school every day and I got it.

In criminal justice, I found out my friend Shubby went to my college, so in between classes while I was on break, we would go to Burger King and get lunch. We switched driving, so we would compensate or else we would have been spending ten dollars a day. This was before Shubby was kicked out for lack of going to class. He might have been up to something else, something not good, but I didn't know nor did I want to know. All I knew is we were best friends and nothing could change that.

On the days we were off, we would walk to this lake in Shubby's neighborhood and go fishing. We must have caught ten bass each, nothing big enough to eat, but the thrill of it kept us going. For a while, he worked at the dollar movie theater and he would get me and a friend in free. It was only a dollar, but even so, it was nice having a friend who worked there. We would also get free popcorn and that was a bonus.

I always thought if I kept busy and didn't let anything interrupt, my hallucinations would go away, but that wasn't the case, and it only made them mad at me. While we were fishing, I saw the water part and Diane was standing in the middle using her hands to part the lake. Shubby was just enjoying fishing, while I'm going through this hell, but I kept fishing and soon it went away, and we kept catching fish.

When I got home it was on a Sunday. On Monday, I had class

and the hallucinations were starting to get a little better, but not much. Diane was showing up on a regular basis, because nothing I did could get her to stop appearing. I didn't like my doctor anymore—I didn't like her tactics. She was a very smart woman with many awards. I respected her, but didn't like her as my doctor. Her vitamins and herbal remedies were useless against what I had—the magnitude of my illness was way past all that crap. I was trapped in purgatory waiting for heaven or hell. I knew I didn't do anything to deserve this hell, so I was a little at ease.

It's like the book, *The Perfect Storm*. I was stuck in the middle of two hurricanes with a flimsy boat that could not take too much more. That boat was my brain and the more flooded it gets with hallucinations, the farther into the abyss I went. Many nights, I laid outside looking at the stars. It was a bit of serenity looking up and trying to count them all when there are stars out, but many nights there aren't any stars. I especially did that when I was depressed. Grandpa Dick would always question why I went out so much, so I just told him I liked looking at the stars. He must have thought I was up to no good. I could see where he was coming from though, going out so many times in the night just looking up at the magnificent night sky.

Whenever I was having hallucinations, which was all the time now, I went out and read under the light on cool nights. I was always glad when the air was cool, because I could have slept out there, it was beautiful. I have always had a fascination with the sky and cool nights. When I was a kid, I would sleep in my tree fort, which now is infested with wasps, but I always told myself if we take care of that, I would sleep in there again. Sure, it's like a kid thing, but if it helps my mood, I'll take that over anything—it was like free medicine.

If I'm depressed, I like artwork or vibrant colors like teal and dark blue. I have a lamp that emits those colors and it really helps more than some medicine does. I could tell what my doctor was doing was wrong, because while seeing her, I had an amazing bout of mania, which I had missed dearly. I was back to life, schoolwork was a breeze, my math was coming easily to me, and I was getting great grades with no problems—just euphoria.

Although my auditory at the time was pretty bad, I barely had any visuals. I even heard Satan talking to me, saying my soul is condemned and he's waiting for me when I died, which was soon he said. I was so scared about going to hell, I was paranoid and didn't know what to do at the time. I didn't want to tell my doctor, because she didn't seem like she understood my illness, especially my hallucinations. I used my mania to the fullest to study, do work, and work out for hours at a time. This time it felt like I consumed a thousand milligrams of caffeine and I never stopped for a minute. Housework became a breeze and I could do anything I wanted again. Energy levels were through the roof, although I only got probably two to three hours of sleep a night, and I would wake up refreshed with lack of sleep.

But again, I knew it would all come to an end, and then the depression would come like a demon staring right through my soul. Diane was still around, even through my mania, just gawking at me everywhere I went and never leaving me alone. At the time I was so manic I didn't give a crap.

At one point, I felt like I could talk to spirits, like I could help them out as much as I could to my best ability. When my mania finally died, I was back to my normal self, but my depression wasn't as bad as before, although it was still there. I would have to try to stay awake and my workouts went in the dumps, but I pushed through as much as I could, because working out with my dad is my life. It's what I look forward to and nothing would get in the way of that. You just have to make the best of it. Knowing I was an intelligent gifted kid with many problems, I just had to try to think of that as a blessing.

I will reiterate that I was never alone. I tried to make friends with my hallucinations and take it from there and sometimes it worked, but that all went down the drain when I saw Diane. She was an evil curse that someone bestowed upon me.

I thought I had a special gift that I was able to communicate with the dead. When I tried to talk to my grandma's urn and she didn't speak back, I thought I could only hear some people voices. What else was I supposed to think—that these were long-lost relatives or the dead coming back to speak through me? I believed it for a while, until I came to my senses.

Then I just looked at it as I was a sick child, who desperately needed help and no one had helped up to this point besides my family. I always felt like an embarrassment to my mom and dad, knowing I was severally mentally ill. I just didn't want to have that on their shoulders. I was afraid that I was a burden and they didn't want me around. I know that's crazy talk, but it's what I felt like. I thought I was an embarrassment to everyone I knew. I knew they were thinking, "That kid's a little off," or "I wonder if he is on drugs?" and stuff like that.

I wasn't, of course, I was just seriously ill. What we were doing at the time wasn't working, but I couldn't tell my doctor that, because she's the one who decided I was having "thought" voices, but I would be able to tell the difference if it was thought or not. She was always saying my illness is all in my head. "Well, no shit—of course, it's in my head—where else would it be, in my butt?" I felt like saying that, but we had no backup plan at the time, so I needed to keep her as long as possible.

It was nice of her to do the Skype interview over the internet and prescribe me Xanax for my anxiety, but that only masked my problem. Two hours later, I was back in the hole with no ladder to help me get out, so I would take one pill every two hours. I liked it a lot, but I knew it wasn't healthy for the body, so I flushed them for the time being. but then I wished I had more pills two hours later. My body craved the pill and my anxiety got worse, but I tried to push through. I felt like I had an eighty-pound weight on my chest and could hardly breathe.

It took a few weeks before I was able to manage my anxiety on my own. It was one of the hardest tests I have ever gone through. I was always worried about my dad because his job was so dangerous, but when he got into Florida Power and Light Power Quality, I could finally rest those fears, because he was a lot safer rather than having to work on high lines. My dad is such a smart tough man that he never got hurt once, except for minor shocks. That was it, but it was enough power for him to throw his hammer out of sight. It must have hurt pretty bad, but for a man who needed two full shoulder replacements, he could handle pain very well. He is the toughest man I have ever known and still is to this day. Somehow he was able to work past the pain, while working out and I couldn't believe how he was still able to bench press—he would even do shoulders.

I was benching one day and when I got up and looked in the mirror like I always do after a set, I saw Diane and her naked body standing behind me. It didn't scare me, because my dad was in there with me, so I just brushed it off and told myself, *I'm safe where I'm at nothing can hurt me.*

Tyler, Dan, and I would work out with each other as much as possible. I was like their personal trainer, before I gained weight and lost the drive to work out, because I was so damn depressed I barely had the strength to work out. My dad, Tyler, and Dan would push me to work out and a little bit into the workout, my endorphins kicked in. The problem for me is that I must have drive. That's what I need to be able to work out.

Luckily in math, I was acing my online homework, because I wasn't good at the test in class. My voices were so loud, I felt like yelling, "Shut the hell up," but that would earn me a ticket home, and it wasn't good in college to be sent home. They would look at your record and possibly say that you couldn't rejoin the class, so I just had to deal with it as much as I could and try not to let it get in my way. I wasn't on any anti psychotics at the time, but I needed to be to get through these classes.

I was in class when I heard another demonic growl. Next to me. I saw this kid looking at me with black ooze coming out of his eyes. That scared me, so I went to the bathroom and looked at myself in the mirror. Behind me, I saw Diane standing closer to me than she had ever been before. She went to talk to me, but I couldn't understand her or what she was saying, because it was in a different language—probably Latin, because all these demonic entities speak in Latin for some reason. I didn't know if I was possessed or something, but I felt like I was possessed by Satan. He was going to take my soul any way possible, but I was fighting him—sort of the most brave will survive, while Diane was staring at me. She put her hand out to take mine and I have never moved quicker in my life to get back to class. I thought, *That was way too close for comfort.*

I liked math class and felt safe in there and the lighting set the mood for happiness, but I don't know why but it did. There was this beautiful girl sitting next to me named Katie. I worked up the courage to see if she wanted to have dinner with me and she said yes. We went to dinner at Outback and then she broke it to me—she had a kid. I didn't want her child to think I was their daddy—that's some stress that would have made my problems worse, so I told her I just wanted to be friends and nothing else. Thank God she understood, plus, I was nineteen and she was thirty.

In my truck on the way home from school, I would try to talk to my voices some more. I would talk to them at other times, but mainly in my truck where I knew no one could see me talking to myself, because I had such dark tinted windows. I even tried to talk to Diane when she was in the truck sitting next to me and sometimes she would answer, but most of the time not.

To be honest, I was hoping she didn't answer, because I would be a bit terrified and I was driving, too. I couldn't do anything else, but race home to my safe sanctuary, which was my room. I always brought my dog or dogs in with me, because I felt safer with them, knowing they would alert me if something was wrong. Almost every night when I slept, I saw the shadow people floating around my bed, so I would cover up in the fetal position and scoot against the wall where I felt they couldn't get me if they tried, but they could have easily gotten me if they wanted.

Finally, the last day of math and criminal justice came. We had our last exam and I aced it, so I didn't have to take the final in criminal justice. I didn't do as well in math, but I got out of there with a C, I was happy about that score, because at least I passed math. I would miss criminal justice, but I was glad to get out with an A.

My next class was Art Appreciation. I loved that class, because artwork makes me happy. We would go over art pieces and study and take tests on them. There were barely any tests though, which I liked. She said if we were to go to the Ringling Art Museum, bring back a wristband that showed we went there, and talk about some artwork, she would boost out grade up by a letter. I loved all the art and sculptures and I got a free letter grade—what more could you want—it was an easy grade. Plus, Grandpa Dick took me, which made the experience even better, because I had someone to talk to in there. The pictures were so real-looking, they seemed 3D like they were coming out of the picture to bring you into their world of majestic art. I wondered if that were what heaven looked like—beautiful colors and majestic art. I wouldn't care if it were like that, as long as I was with my family and some friends.

In art class, I would still see Diane and a new visual of this guy in a black suit and no face just pale skin I called him, Bruce. I don't know why I named them, but it helped me keep track of who I was seeing. Our art teacher's name was Miss Hill. I saw Bruce standing behind her, stroking her hair. I could see it moving every time he stroke it and I thought to myself, *Why the hell doesn't she feel that?* So I just brushed it off, pardon the pun. Bruce was always messing with Miss Hill by putting his hand on her shoulder and again brushing her hair and punching through her chest exposing her heart, but there was nothing I could do besides wait for it to be over.

Just like Diane, I was starting to see Bruce everywhere, even while I was showering, but at least she was a woman. I didn't like knowing a guy was walking in on me naked, even though he was not real. A guy in a black suit with no face, eyes, ears, nose, or mouth, and all that I could focus on is, *I wonder what his face would look like if he were to have a face.* When he would turn around, he has black wings like a fallen angel, so I knew it was demonic, because I could tell the way he acted and the things he would say to me like, "Hell is your new heaven. We will reign down upon this earth and take you for our slave." That scared me every time he would say it, even though it was just a hallucination. I really thought I was destined for hell.

When I would stay the night at Tyler's house, we would go to Starbucks and sit and drink coffee knowing it was going to be a long night riding around and watching movies. I would get a triple espresso, but it wouldn't amp me up like my mania would. We loved watching scary movies, even though I was living a scary movie. I thought, What harm could it do, if I'm already seeing this evil sinister stuff—what else could go wrong? I was right though, because nothing else did go wrong, but I was having problems anyway.

I remember this movie called *The Grudge*. It scared the hell out of me, because it looked like some of the images in the movie is what I was seeing in real life, plus, I would see the girl from the movie standing next to me and on the screen. I would switch seats with Tyler and make him sit next to the closet with me sitting next to the wall. If she couldn't get to me there, I was safe. I would hear the noise she would make though and it scared the living hell out of me, but as long as I was with Tyler watching it with him next to me, I once again felt safe. I had to go use his bathroom, but I hated that his shower curtain was always closed, so I hurried to open it up. When I did, I saw Bruce hanging by the nozzle, so I quickly did my business and ran to the chill room where we were watching *The Grudge* and sat down, somewhat panting, but he didn't notice and I didn't want him to notice. That would have been a hard thing to try to get him to understand.

I was upset when art appreciation was over, but my next class was psychology, which I loved dearly. It was so interesting and intriguing, I could never put my book down and stop reading. It was a six-week course, so it was fast-paced, but I was going through hypomania at the time, so again, everything came easy to me. God picked a good time for me to be manic, because I needed it. Every week, we had a one-hundred question test, which I always aced, but it did take a lot of studying to be able to get that easy grade and easy it was—it just took time and you have to love what you're taking for it to become that easy.

Our instructor, Miss Green, was a hefty black lady with a deep voice like a man, but I liked her a lot, because she was determined not to let one person fail her class. When they would have a blood drive at school, I tried to give blood, but they turned me down for having lithium in my blood, which I had forgotten about, but I could have made someone seriously ill. Plus, I had to get out of there, because there sat Bruce getting his blood taken. Why couldn't they see him right in front of their eyes? It must have been another kid that Bruce was posing as, so I went to the Smoothie King in the school and got a Chocolate Hulk. It's a protein shake that I slowly slurped before my psychology class. When I went in and took my seat, I was the only one in room at the time, so I knew something was bound to happen. Amazingly, nothing happened as the students started to come in and then the instructor. I was taking my test, when I saw blood dripping onto my paper. When I looked up, I saw Bruce hanging from the ceiling, blood dripping from his mouth or where his mouth was supposed to be. I closed my eyes and asked for it to go away and when I opened my eyes, I was back to normal, so I finished my test, turned it in, and got the hell home to safety.

I had psychology three times a week, too, so we would go in there, get the material we had to study, go home, and study our butts off. Every now and then, she let us have open book tests and that was an easy 100%, because all of it was right in front of you.

I had a very frightening hallucination of a small girl with me in my truck saying, "Help me, it hurts!" When I asked what hurts, she said, "My belly." I asked why and when she showed me her belly, there was a big knife wound gash, so I looked at the road and raced home as quickly and safely as possible. I could still see her out of the corner of my eyes, so I just kept my eyes on the road. By the time I was halfway home, she was gone.

That startled me a bit, because seeing small kids in my visuals is always freaky. That was a mix between a visual and auditory. I couldn't believe they were talking to me. I thought, *Man, I'll never have to make a friend again, because they're with me all the time, day and night. They can't backstab you like a friend could, because it was all in my hallucinations.* I just had to try to make the best of it even though that was impossible.

Nothing else really happened in psychology, besides my daily routine of seeing Diane and Bruce, but after I got out of that class with an A, next came reading class. I don't remember much about it, because I was so out of it, I remember being on Haldol at this point, which dulled my senses and made me shake like hell. My mother would have to write most of my papers for me with my help, but I couldn't help much with the state I was in, almost like a trance. I didn't know really how to help, but I did as good as I could. I was always achy and shaky and my vision was also blurred. I was still having hallucinations and thought to myself, *Why go through this, if it's not working?*

I didn't even know the alphabet and I couldn't recite it, nor remember it. I had forgotten how to write cursive, which is the only writing style I ever learned. I never ever learned how to write in printing—just cursive. My mom would pretty much do all my work for me I was just too out of it I don't even remember helping, but I guess, I did a little but she knew something was wrong with me, because I don't even remember if I knew my own damn name. I was a walking zombie, except for the eating of brains part.

My hallucinations were still there, though I was so drugged up on several medications. I forget my instructor's name, but she was a nice lady and cared for her students. Luckily for me, we had to bring our work home and work on it at home and then, take it to her the next day. That's where my mom came in to help me as much as possible. I had a plethora of ideas running through my head on what I would write and how to write it, but every idea passed by so fast, I couldn't grab it and use it. Then as fast as it came, I would forget it—gone with no recollection of anything. I couldn't help but shake.

I do remember one day, she pulled me aside after class and asked if I was okay and why was I shaking—I just told her I had a anxiety problem. Then she threatened me with a drug test and I said, "Hell, yes, drug test me! I don't have anything to hide." After I said that, she told me she believed me, so I had no drug test, but I didn't care—I knew I was clean. It pissed me off that she would even threaten me like that, but I guess I could see where she was coming from. I mean, I was shaky, glassy-eyed, and constantly looking around the room to see if my hallucinations were playing a trick on me. I wasn't mad at her after I went through that in my mind. I would have probably done the same thing if I were she.

There were some kids in there that would have absolutely failed the drug test. They just didn't act as suspicious like I did. They were smart about their drug use, if there even is such a thing to be smart and still do drugs, although there are some kids out there that surprise me on their smarts while on drugs. It's baffling, but it can be done.

I was never for drugs and never wanted to be, even with all the crap I was going through, I would kill to have a normal day or what normal people call a normal day, without paranoia, anxiety, hallucinations, and delusions. I hadn't felt normal in my life, even before this illness took control of me. All I want is a normal day and even take away my hair-pulling Trichotillomania.

Even on some days where my hallucinations weren't giving me any problems, I still had other issues, including mainly the paranoia, which was the worst. I was basically looking over my shoulder to see if my hallucinations were following me or even just being there. If I were to have a good day, I would call it being sober and if my problems came back, I would call that a relapse.

Even with the medication I was on, I still didn't have that many sober times. Hell, I thought, if I could just have a sober day or even two hours, that would be an amazing feat for me. If I was having auditory only without any visuals, I would even called that a sober day, but that rarely happened. When it was either one or the other, if I have to pick between them, I would gladly take auditory, because the visuals were quite frightening, even though the auditory ones are, too, and I couldn't see anyone talking, so it made things worse. If I was charged one hundred grand to have a normal day, I would gladly find a way to pay that just to see what a normal person sees, hears, and feels.

I studied the emotions and reactions of all the people in my class. They all seemed so happy and full-on out there, but I was stuck in purgatory. Why me? I don't know or understand why a normal good person had to be plagued with such a nasty illness, where I couldn't have a normal day, even on medication. The mood stabilizers had controlled my bipolar somewhat, my rage was gone, and my mania disappeared. I always wondered why I couldn't keep my mania and get rid of my hallucinations, but if I did that, the lack of sleep would open up so many more issues, like immune system problems. I don't see how it could get any worse.

All I knew is I was stuck between both worlds, good and evil. The good was seeing angels occasionally and the evil, which was almost all the time, was seeing Diane, Bruce, and demons and demonic pictures. I would see them in my head and projected onto a wall or ceiling pretty much everywhere. The angels made me feel at peace, like it was safe, so I welcomed them into my head, but it didn't last long. I always feel safe with my parents. My mom takes me for golf cart rides around the neighborhood like the good old times, but it was better when I got older, because I appreciated the vibrant colors and tried to leave my problems behind me, while up ahead I would see Diane or Bruce. They seemed to come a couple minutes apart from each other. As we would pass, I could see their heads slowly turn to look at me, just staring through my soul and ready to take me away to wherever they were from. I was just so tired, I really didn't care.

I knew I was a Christian and knew God had good plans for me. Maybe he's trying to test me to see how much I can handle before I finally cave in. I was determined never to give in to my illness. I'm a tough guy, so I will never give in to my illness. It's my bitch, but I will never be its bitch.

After writing class, I had speech, which was very hard for me, because I was not a social person at all. However, I still got up there and said what I had to say, even though in the background, I would hear little girls' voices, so I had to stop frequently and try to remember where I was at. I knew they probably thought I was on something, because I was shaking like a liver, but I didn't care. As long as I could get through that class, I was happy.

We had to give a speech about our lives, which made me think, Oh my God I'm going to have to tell them, but I didn't know how to say it, so I didn't. I just told them how I grew up and my struggles in growing up and how I prospered. Even though my parents knew what I had, which was still bipolar psychosis, but I knew that it was something else, because I was having too many problems for it just to be that. I still didn't tell them everything, because it was so evil, I didn't know whether I should keep it a secret or not, but I finally told them. Pretty much everything kept going bad for me until about a year later ,I met my doctor, which I still have now. He is a very smart guy and I wouldn't trade doctors for all the world. I like him so much, because he knew so much about my illness. However, even with him, we had trial and error with many different antipsychotics. We tried to give them enough time as possible to find the perfect "cocktail," as he called it, which was brilliant.

It was at this point, I met my friend, Garrett. He was a good friend with the exact same problem I have. I finally got my real diagnosis, which was bipolar type schizoaffective, which is bipolar and schizophrenia mixed, so I get the worst of both worlds. I read that one in ten thousand get schizoaffective. I must have failed every single antipsychotic out there, but we kept trying, before I went on the medicine I am on now today.

I picked my doctor myself, through a friend who was seeing him and thought I will give this doctor a try and finally had a first visit and loved his work ever since. Garrett and I were hanging out every day, while Tyler was in Jacksonville and Dan was in rehab. We would go for walks to the gas station to get energy drinks and candy bars. Garrett was with us at JoTos when I turned twenty-one and had my first beer at my neighbor's house—after dinner. Of course, I had to get the most potent beer out there with an alcohol content of 12, which is almost three beers in a bottle, but I was all about the buzz at the time. I didn't care if it tastes like butt, because I would still have drunk it just to get that feeling.

My favorite all-time beer was Blue Moon with an orange in it. I also enjoy Bud Light Platinum with an alcohol content of 6. I didn't like it for the buzz, but because I just really liked the taste.

One hallucination I had and still have to this day is a lady with black hair holding two trash bags, just standing and staring at me. I always wanted to know what was in the bags, but then I realized that it was probably for the best not to know what was in there. I called her Debby, so I had Bruce with no face, Diane the naked body, and now Debby with the trash bags. Those are the only hallucination I named, because they would follow me everywhere I went. Luckily, Garrett lives close to me, because driving home late at night having hallucinations is not safe, especially with Debby standing in the middle of the road with those damn trash bags. I would drive right through her, but what if it was a real person that I could have hit?

The scariest night was when I was driving home from his house and Debby was standing in the middle of the road with her bags. Bruce was next to me and Diane was in the back seat, so I thought, *This can't be good.* It was pitch black and the streetlights barely worked, but it offered enough light for me to see Debby. At this time, I was straightforward with my parents. I had told them everything I was seeing, when and where, and if I was doing anything to cause them, like alcohol. It wasn't that, because I would mainly just go to the bar called Smoking Joes, which Tyler introduced me to. I loved going there to play pool and have a beer.

The guy was selling cigars when I saw Diane standing behind him fully nude, just listening to what he had to say, so I turned around. Now the bartender was gone and in her place was Bruce holding a bottle and pouring a drink for one of the customers. On the outside of the door, I saw Debby with her trash bags, just staring through my soul, but I didn't care. I was in a populated bar with Tyler, so I felt a little bit more comfortable, than I would if I were by myself. Tyler and I were a team and we would play so much pool that the people we were playing would offer to buy the winner. We would whop them and get a free game of pool, so we must have played twenty games that night.

About halfway through my 21st birthday, my parents thought I was starting to develop a habit and asked me if I would quit drinking. I kindly agreed to stop, because it's not fun trying to chase a high that costs money. All I have to do is stop taking my medicine and I would be as high as a kite, and that would be a natural high, without putting harm on the body. No matter how much I wanted to, I never ever quit taking my meds, even for a couple days, because I know my family and my doctor would be pissed and mainly, because I knew what would happen—the downfall would be worse than the bubonic plaque.

I went to visit Tyler at his house in Jacksonville. It was a nice house and he had three roommates, which I liked, but not that much. I had to cart my medicine around with me and try to remember to take them at exactly the same time every night or the next day would be hell, but I never missed or forgot a dose. It's like feeding a baby, where you have a set time, unless the baby is hungry. I couldn't do that, but all I could do is take my meds within a 12-hour period, one dose in the morning and one dose at night.

For a while, I thought my hallucinations were over, or at least while I was at his house, but they weren't over. I was getting out of the shower, but when I pulled the curtain back, I saw Diane and her naked body hanging from the shower pole so I looked in the mirror and still saw her hanging. I dried off and ran to the living room, where we watched *Family Guy* to try to get some joy out of the situation. I had already told Tyler what I was going through, but he had to have known, because no normal person carries around so many pills unless they seriously mentally ill or diabetic. I asked him to keep it a secret and he has kept that secret ever since.

I also told his parents, because they are like my second family. Tyler's dad reads a lot of books or listens to them as he cuts grass, so they researched my issues, after they knew what I had to get more knowledge about my disease.

It sucks for me to try to concentrate extremely hard on someone talking, with all the voices going on inside my head. If its two people talking, I can't hear both of them at once. I have to focus on one person only and then listen to the second person who is talking. I knew they must have thought I was ignoring them, but I wasn't. I just couldn't focus on two people.

It was funny, because Tyler, his family, and I were at a Texas Road House for dinner and I was hearing the *Terminator* theme song. I felt like a badass, because I felt like the Terminator was everywhere I walked and the theme would follow me and become louder and louder. Finally, I went to the bathroom and told it to shut the hell up, I couldn't take it anymore. Debby was behind me, of course, so I asked, "Why the hell are you following me?"

Her response was, "Because you are condemned to hell." I just ignored her, and washed my hands, and went back to dinner. That night, Tyler and I watched this movie called *Dead Silence*, very good movie, but probably not the best choice for a guy who was hallucinating all this sinister, evil, visuals and horrible auditory.

As I said before though, I love it, I love the rush of fear, although nothing really scared me at this point anymore, because I was living it without having to watch a scary movie to make me jump. Whenever Tyler and I would go to see a scary movie at the movies, he was always wondering why I never jumped and I would say if you're living it, then nothing really scares you anymore, although when I see Diane, Bruce, or Debby, I still do tend to be a little startled.

I mainly saw Debby at Garrett's house, either while we were watching a movie or on the ride home, she was always there. We didn't watch many scary movies at his house, but mainly TV shows like *Dexter*, or *Breaking Bad* and *Ink Master*. *Dexter* was our favorite, but I was on the edge of his bed and I would see hands crawling up next to me, trying to grab me, and yank me under the bed. I would just stay attached to the show and try to show no fear, while I tried to convince myself that if they wanted me dead, I would be dead already. All I would tell myself is that these are not real, so they can't hurt you, because they are not there—it's just my brain playing tricks on me.

It took me a while to realize that they could not hurt me, but once I found out how to talk to them, I felt a lot better, because I would tell them to shut up. I also would go into the bathroom and wash my face and then go back to the bed. When I stayed the night, Garrett would let me sleep in his bed and he would sleep on the couch. I felt so much safer in his room with the door cracked open, so I could see out the door and see him lying there and I know that I was safe.

At this time, Tyler had moved down from Jacksonville and into a small house about five miles from mine. I was so happy to have my best friend back. We would be together all the time and walk to Smoking Joes to have a few drinks and play more pool and I also watched *Breaking Bad* at his house.

That only lasted a couple months and then he broke it to me that he was going to move to North Carolina. It was very upsetting for me, because I would rarely get to see him if he moved up there. Before long, he was gone, but he did promise me that he would come down as much as possible and keep a good connection with me on the phone, which we did and still do. Garrett and his family were planning on moving, too, although they only moved about six miles away from me. It still sucks, because we couldn't walk to the gas station anymore without crossing six lanes of traffic.

Certified Nurse Assistant (CNA)

I WAS WONDERING WHAT I COULD DO FOR ANOTHER
job, so I asked my mom how she liked the Certified Nurse
Assistant program. She said she loved it, so I thought, *Why not?
I might as well try.* My first class was Medical Terminology. I got
out of that class with an A and then came the class with 120
hours of it and I fell in love right away. I was certified in cardio
pulmonary resuscitation (CPR) and First Aid. CPR was fun to
practice on a dummy and also, because now I know if it came
down to it, I knew what to do. My teacher, Mrs. Walker, is a
registered nurse, so she knew her work, what to do, and how to
do it. I was always nervous to perform in front of the class, but
took it like a champ. I just went up there, did what I had to do,
and sat down. I went to the bathroom and when I came back,
all the dummies were sitting up and staring at me. If I walked to
the side, they would refocus their eyes on me, and if I walked the
other way, they would follow me. I felt like making them dance,
but I knew the whole class would be afraid of me if I were to do
that.

After class, I had to wait a couple weeks to go on this website
to sign up for my CNA test. I studied my butt off and failed it
the first time, so the second time, I practiced my clinicals with
my mom and dad and watched internet videos to get the best
knowledge I could, *before* taking the next test. Mrs. Walker gave
me a few pointers on how to pass it, and before class ended, she

would bring me after school and help with clinicals. My nerves got the best of me for my first test, so by the time it got to the second one, I was ready for it. I passed both my computer exam and my clinical skills, scoring 100% on my clinicals, which are the most important of all.

Since my mom is a nurse practitioner, she was able to hook me up with a lot of nursing homes and assisted living homes. One that stood out the most to me is a place called Desoto Palms. It's a beautiful three-story facility, so I thought, *Oh man, this is the one for me!* I went in and applied and got the job—I was so excited! Since this was the first job I've ever had in the medical field, I was nervous as hell, but made it through to my first day.

Soon I had to work two stories, which was insane, because I would have to take care of forty people at a time. If I had trouble, I always had my walkie talkie, but I didn't like to break radio silence. I was embarrassed, because if I break radio silence, all staff in the building would all hear me and I was worried what my voice sounded like.

Some residents needed to be in a nursing home, rather than an assisted living facility. One resident didn't know her name or what year it was. Transporting her here was horrible, because deep down, I knew she had to know some of what was happening. Lots of the residents were mean as hell, trying to hit the staff. This one lady that I had to feed would spit occasionally, but she didn't really do it to be mean. She told me she likes me and that was nice to hear.

Then out of the blue, my hallucinations came back with a vengeance. I was seeing Bruce standing at the end of hallways, Diane in residents' rooms, and Debby I saw everywhere I went. I hated to be in a room by myself, because I was too afraid to stay and I'll admit it. I had a pretty funny visual, I saw dolphins on pogo sticks jumping by, looking right at me, and I kind of laughed. My trainer at the time gave me a half-smile, half mean look. she was probably puzzled, because there wasn't anything around to make us laugh.

I was in a resident's room one day, helping him get his socks off, when his TV turned to static and Debby was there on the screen, holding her trash bags and just staring at me. I asked, "What is wrong with the TV and all the static?"

The resident goes, "What are you talking about?"

I said, "The TV isn't working," but when I turned back, it was normal again, with no more Debby. When I turned back to him, he said, "Maybe you should see the nurse." I got the hell out of there.

I worked the three to eleven shift, which was good, because it was somewhat quiet until after dinnertime. Then it was chaos, with residents wanting to go to their room or be put to bed for the night. After that, it was quiet, unless they had to use the bathroom and couldn't do it by themselves. I always said to myself, "This is someone's mom or dad or grandma or grandpa, so I took care of them the best I could."

A few months before starting at Desoto Palms, I was put on the medicine I'm still to this day taking, called Clozapine, which was the only medicine that helped me get through this crisis with minimal problems, although I still had some trouble. I would try to take it a half hour before my shift was over, because it's a heavy sedater. Also, I was on several different medications at the time, so I had to make sure I was able to drive home, but I had a couple of scares like seeing Debby again standing in the middle of the road.

The final straw that made me quit was when I was standing in the elevator and it caught on fire. I was trapped and I could even feel the heat, so I slammed on the alarm. It rang loudly and when it opened, I ran the hell out of there. A black girl ran up asking who set the alarm off, so I pointed down the hallway saying, "I think he or she went down there somewhere."

I was extremely depressed most of the time there and everyone knew it. I would get called down to the nurse, asking if I was okay and I would say yes, just hoping I could get fired, but then I thought to myself, *Give it your all and if you get fired, that limits your options for ever getting hired again by any place.*

I forget how it happened, but I finally came out and said I was Type 1 bipolar and that I needed a medical leave. They granted it for me, so I wrote a letter saying how much I respected the place and how much I liked the employees and that was it for Desoto Palms. It's true though, I liked pretty much everyone that worked there, as they were respectful, kind, and caring, but I just couldn't take the torment anymore.

My Future

A FEW MONTHS LATER I WAS PUT ON MELLARIL, AS well as Clozapine and my mood stabilizers, so things got a little better. my body is still adjusting to it but things have settles down a bit not as much as I hope but it's getting better each day. I still see Bruce, Debby, and Diane, but I have gotten used to them and my meds are kicking their asses. Every day is a journey for me.

I continue to wonder why this happens to people and if there will ever be cure. My doctor, Dr. Barrow, keeps a close eye on me to watch my moods and my hallucinations, but my parents are the ones who know my every move and the way I'm acting and why I'm acting like that.

Unfortunately, my doctor is not able to see my moods, because he's not with me every day. However, Dr. Barrow is a great doctor and I would not change doctors for the world. I am thrown into the abyss and every day, I go through some torment, but the journey through madness continues, as I try my best to conquer it and hope for a cure.

I'm hoping this helps people as much as it has helped me. You must have a great support system, with a loving family and friends. That's how we can defeat this disease by having this much-needed support.

I wish for a cure someday and I'm willing to wait a long time. Even if it takes a decade or more, I just want all this to be over and not look back with regret. My struggle has made me a stronger person, because if I can handle this I can handle the world. I just have to stay as strong as possible and pray every day that there will be light at the end of this very long tunnel.

CPSIA information can be obtained
at www.ICGtesting.com
Printed in the USA
FFOW03n0539271116
29712FF